The Wise Owl Guide to…
# DANTES Subject Standardized Test (DSST)

---

# Substance Abuse (Formerly Drug and Alcohol Abuse)

Second Edition

ISBN-10: 1440486530
ISBN-13: 9781440486531

Library of Congress Control Number: 2009912021

Cover design © Wise Owl Publications, LLC

This book is not affiliated with Prometric.

## Introduction

Are you going to learn everything about substance abuse in this study guide? Absolutely not! But…are you going to learn enough to pass the DSST test? YES! In this book we focus on what you need to know, that is it. With the DSST (Dantes Subject Standardized Test) series tests, the test is on what is most commonly taught in a college course. That leaves out a lot of content of what could be taught. Expect to see some answers that you don't know. But, the goal isn't to get 100% (you should take a traditional class and invest lots of time, money, and effort to do that). The goal here is simply to pass. Prepare for this test with this study guide and you will be well on your way to a degree in significantly less time than hitting the books in night school (this is not to say it is any easier to get a degree this way, just more flexible)! This book is written in an easy to read, understand, and remember format. Substance abuse is a fascinating real-world topic, and whether you have a test to pass or not this information will make you feel like a more educated person for knowing it. Even if you think you know everything there is to know about substance abuse, this book will teach you a thing or two!

Substance Abuse Dantes Subject Standardized Test (DSST) test covers similar material that is taught in a three-credit college upper-level (social science) course.

The exam (and this book) covers topics such as:

- Overview of Substance Abuse and Dependence Abuse
- Drug Classification
- Pharmacological and Neuropsychological Principles
- Alcohol
- Anti-anxiety and Sedative Hypnotics
- Inhaled Substances
- Tobacco and Nicotine
- Psychomotor Stimulants
- Opioids
- Cannabinoids
- Hallucinogens
- Other Drugs of Abuse
- Anti-psychotic Drugs
- Antidepressants and Mood Stabilizers

This test book includes a 100-question practice test to ensure you have a solid handle on the course information.

## PART I. OVERVIEW OF SUBSTANCE ABUSE AND DEPENDENCE ABUSE

This test is divided among many areas of substance abuse. This portion of the test will account for approximately eleven percent of the questions. Part I will cover:

- Terminology
- Theories of Abuse and Dependence
- Models of Abuse and Dependence
- Demographics
- Costs to society and associations with social problems
- Screening and Diagnosis

### TERMINOLOGY

While the glossary of this study guide is robust, it is important to review some of the most basic definitions of drugs early in the study guide to provide greater understanding of the text.

- **Drug** – any substance that modifies the bodily functions (yes that includes coffee!).
- **Psychoactive drugs** – substances that specifically affect the central nervous system, consciousness, and perceptions.
- **Licit drugs** – legal substances that affect bodily functions (coffee, alcohol, tobacco).
- **Illicit drugs** – illegal substances that affect bodily functions (cocaine, marijuana, and others).
- **Over-the-counter drugs (OTC)** – drugs sold without a prescription.
- **Gateway drugs** – substances that typically lead to more severe drugs and heavier usage. The three gateway drugs are alcohol, tobacco, and marijuana.
- **Medicines** – drugs used to treat or prevent an illness, prescribed by a medical doctor.
- **Floaters / Chippers** – light to moderate consumption of drugs (vacillating between chronic and experimental use).
- **Teetotaler** – someone who does not drink alcohol for any reason.

Some of the most commonly abused drugs are:

- **Cannabis (Marijuana, Hashish)** – the dried leaves, flowers, stems, and seeds of the Cannabis Sativa Plant. Either inhaled (through a pipe or cigarette) or ingested (typically through baking batter).
- **Stimulants** – substances that affect the central nervous system by increasing alertness, restlessness, insomnia, and pulse rate. Examples of stimulants are cocaine, crack, amphetamines, coffee, tea, and tobacco.

Other forms of drugs that are categorized based on their effects or chemical make-up are:

- **Hallucinogens** – alter perceptions (also known as psychedelics).
  - Examples are: lysergic acid diethylamide (LSD), mescaline, and peyote.
- **Depressants** – sedatives that are used to relieve stress and/or induce sleep.
  - Examples are: barbiturates, benzodiazepines (Valium), methaqualone (Quaalude), and alcohol (ethanol).
- **Narcotics** – drugs that depress the central nervous system (CNS).
  - Examples are: opium derivatives, morphine, codeine, and heroin.
- **Inhalants** – typically used by the adolescent population, household products that are very dangerous to inhale to achieve a state of euphoria ("high").
  - Products used include: gasoline, airplane glue, and paint thinner.
- **Designer drugs** – drugs designed to mimic the effects of illicit drugs and controlled substances.

There are different forms of drug use; the types are drugs misuse, drug abuse, and drug addiction.

- **Drug misuse** – the unintentional misuse of prescribed or over-the-counter drugs (i.e., taking more than prescribed, stopping a medicine before prescribed, or sharing medicines).
- **Drug abuse** – the intentional misuse of any drug.
- **Drug addiction** – a physiological and psychological need for drug abuse.

There are four ways that drug users experience consumption of drugs:

- **Pharmacological**
  - o Ingredient's effect on body and social behavior.
- **Cultural**
  - o Society's view on the drug use (acceptance, non-acceptance).
- **Social**
  - o User's motivation for drug consumption (e.g., pain, illness, relaxation, or stress).
- **Contextual**
  - o Personal disposition to the drug use (i.e., is the drug taken only during parties or social settings or at home in secret).

There are several theories that attempt to explain drugs abuse and dependence (why drug use affects some people). The theories are:

- Biological
- Psychological
- Social

## BIOLOGICAL

The **biological explanation** focuses heavily on the reward sensors found in the CNS (they are more sensitive in a user's CNS to their drug of choice). Other people that find the effects of the same drug unpleasant will not typically abuse the drug. The biological theory also subscribes to the belief that drugs alter the brain chemistry interfering with the **neurotransmitters'** (chemical brain messengers') functioning.

- The American Psychological Association (APA) classifies drug abuse as a mental condition because of several reasons that seem to support the biological explanation of drug use:
  - o Psychiatric disorders and drug abuse seem to occur simultaneously.

- Therapies that are successful in the treatment of mental illnesses have also been found to help with drug abusers.
- Sometimes people that are abusing drugs seem to be self-medicating to relieve symptoms of a mental health disorder.

- The biological explanation supports that drug abuse can be an inherited trait (**genetic**). The genetic belief is supported by the following:
    - Psychiatric disorders caused by genetics may be relieved by drug abuse (thus encouraging use).
    - Some people's reward centers are more sensitive than others'.
    - Character traits that make drug abuse likely (vulnerability, for example) can be inherited.
    - The strength of the withdrawal effects can be genetic, making it more difficult for some to cease use.

### PSYCHOLOGICAL

The **psychological explanation** focuses heavily on abusers' inability to cope with reality and their desire to escape. The psychological theory states that drugs are a psychological problem based on the following facts:

- It is difficult to tell the difference between primary mental disorders and a drug that is exhibiting the same symptoms. Sometimes the only way to do so is to give a test, and examine personal and family histories.
- Receiving acceptance from a peer group reinforces abuse.
- Users repeat the patterns of abuse until they are well established (**habituation**).
    - **Bejerot's addiction to pleasure theory** opines that abuse is a learned behavior, and therefore it is possible to relearn a new behavior. According to Bejerot, the five factors that cause the increase risk of an individual in drugs abuse are:

- Availability of the drug.
- Means to procure the drug.
- Time to use the drug.
- Example of the use of the drug in the environment.
- Permissive ideology in using the drug.

### SOCIAL

The **social explanation** focuses heavily on approval or, oppositely, disapproval. The ratio between favorable and unfavorable using behavior (**differential reinforcement**) is based on:

- Peer groups drug use
- Community drug preference
- Age of users
- Frequency of drug use by peers

Some important notes when understanding the impact of society on drug users are:

- The **labeling theory** stresses that other people's impression of us has a direct impact on our self-image.

- **Primary deviance** is when someone is engaging in a small deviant behavior but does not identify with it. For example, someone experimenting with drugs does not identify him- or herself as a "user."

- **Secondary deviance** is when someone begins to identify him- or herself with the deviant behavior. For example, someone may start to perceive him- or herself as a drug user and will more likely become an abuser.

- **Master status** is an overriding position in the eyes of others. This can be a positive one (doctor, lawyer, police officer) or a negative one (mental patient, alcoholic, "druggie").

## MODELS OF ABUSE AND DEPENDENCE

There are five main models for substance abuse. The models are moral, temperance, disease, psychological, and social.

### MORAL MODEL

The moral model is focused on the abuser breaking society's rules. People that subscribe to the moral model believe the abuser made a conscious choice to abuse drugs. Therefore, the deviance is punishable and the abuser is responsible for his or her choice to use drugs. The moral model is a popular belief among the religious community. In the moral model the intervention focuses around spiritual guidance, moral persuasion, and consequences (imprisonment).

### TEMPERANCE MODEL

The temperance model is often confused with the moral model. The Prohibition Movement in the late 19th century was an example of temperance. Subscribers to the temperance model believe that the idea of moderation is impractical and therefore abstinence is the only other option.

### DISEASE MODEL

About the same time that Prohibition was repealed in the United States a new viewpoint (the disease model) emerged that drug abuse was a unique, irreversible, and progressive disease. The belief is that people abuse drugs because they are biologically "programmed" to do so. For example, alcoholism and addiction are not curable; however, they can be treated. The cause of such a disease in this model is the belief that people inherit abnormal traits. The treatment for the disease is the identification and lifelong abstinence of the drug. Many people participate in peer groups (such as Alcoholics Anonymous and Narcotics Anonymous) to seek treatment for the condition.

### PSYCHOLOGICAL (CHARACTEROLOGICAL) MODEL

Proponents of the psychological model believe that there are certain characteristics within a personality that make a person more susceptible to drug abuse. The chemical dependence develops as a symptom of the person's needs, motives, and attitudes. The psychological model suggests that people have an "addictive personality" that has the following common traits:

- Poor impulse control
- Low self-esteem
- Poor coping mechanisms
- Narcissistic
- Manipulative
- Need for power

The treatment usually consists of therapy.

### SOCIAL MODEL

The social model focuses on drug use being a learned behavior, much like the schools of classical and operant conditioning. The social model outlines the causes of drug abuse as:

- Poor socialization
- Poor modeling
- Lacking coping mechanisms

The treatment under the social model is to correct the socialization, modeling, and coping mechanisms through peer modeling and behavioral counseling.

Drug use crosses income, social class, race, and age boundaries. The experimenters (typically using marijuana, tobacco, and alcohol) typically use for recreation, peer pressure, and curiosity purposes. Compulsive users cannot enjoy life without getting high; when not high, the preoccupation of the drug is all consuming.

Drug abusers typically have several common characteristics:

- Gateway drugs preceding the harder drugs.
- **Amotivational syndrome** (lack of interest in any goals), which is typical of a marijuana smoker.
- Insecurity and immaturity.
- Use of drugs before the age of 12 with poor school behavior and performance.
- Deviant activities and a value system that condones deviance.
- Peer setting where drug use is common.
- A home life with distant, divorced, or dual working parents.
- No significant root system (moving frequently).
- Minorities wishing to offset the perceived powerlessness of their place in society.
- Drug pushers that believe the drug business is a successful entrepreneurship opportunity.

The reasons that people become drug abusers vary widely, including:

- Pleasure
- Stress relief
- Peer pressure
- Religious enhancement
- Pain relief

## COSTS TO SOCIETY AND ASSOCIATIONS WITH SOCIAL PROBLEMS

It is of little question that drug use comes at a great cost to society, including:

- Broken homes
- Illnesses
- Shortened lives

In order to sustain a very expensive drug habit many users are unable to work and resort to theft, pimping, or prostitution to pay for their next fix. Society pays for the prisons that hold drug abusers, the babies that result from drugged-out mothers and the increase of HIV and AIDS in society. Additionally, corporations lose billions of dollars worth of productivity from people with drugs issues, including:

- Alcohol abuse
- Cigarettes (smoking breaks)
- Marijuana use
- Smokeless tobacco
- Non-medical use of prescription drugs

Society makes rules and regulations to try to shield people from:

- Addiction
- Drugs that cause harm (e.g., Phen-Fen)

Some of the general law enforcement and community involvement strategies that society uses to prevent drug abuse are:

- Reducing the supply of illegal drugs.
- Interdicting the supply lines of drugs.
- Attempting to reduce the demand for drugs by refocusing and retraining youth to not want drugs.
- Inoculation strategies by teaching drug users how to survive without the use of drugs.

## Screening and Diagnosis

The most common illicit drugs in descending order of use are:

- Marijuana
- Stimulants
- Hallucinogens
- Narcotics
- Depressants
- Organic Solvents

The five phases of drug addiction are:

- Relief
- Increased use of substance
- Preoccupation with acquiring and using the substance
- Dependency
- Withdrawal from substance

The career pattern of addiction has six steps that have varying degrees of visible symptoms among family and peers:

- Experimentation (initiation into the drug world)
- Escalation (increased use of drugs)
- Maintenance (maintaining the drug use)
- Dysfunction (unsuccessful attempts to quit and a constant use of the drug)
- Recovery (getting out of the drug life)
- Ex-addict (successful termination of drug use)

There are several levels of addiction, and the lower the level the harder it is to identify (and the more likely that the person is not suffering from a serious drug issue):

- Level 0
    - Total abstinence
    - No drug use of any kind, not even for recreational purposes

- Level 1
    - Rarely use, and likely only during recreation
- Level 2
    - Social use and signs of an early problem with drug abuse
- Level 3
    - Heavy drug use
    - Early addiction
    - Person is dependent
- Level 4
    - Significantly dependent on drugs
    - Medical consequences

PART II. CLASSIFICATION OF DRUGS

The government created a classification system of drugs that categorizes drugs into five schedules. The Drug Enforcement Administration (DEA) and the Food and Drug Administration (FDA) determine the schedules for drug use. This portion of the test will account for six percent of the total questions. The qualifications for drug placement are as follows:

- Schedule I
    - High potential for abuse
    - No accepted medical use
    - Lack of safety
    - Examples (not all inclusive) of Schedule I:
        - Heroin
        - Lysergic acid diethylamide (LSD)
        - Gamma hydroxybutyrate acid (GHB)
        - 3, 4- methylenedioxymethamphetamine (MDMA, Ecstasy)
- Schedule II
    - High potential for abuse
    - Accepted medical use with severe restrictions
    - Abuse may lead to psychological or physical dependence
    - Substances are only available (legally) via prescription
        - The prescriptions are monitored by the DEA
    - Examples (not all inclusive) of Schedule II:
        - Ritalin (treatment of Attention Deficit Disorder)
        - Methadone (for heroin treatment)
        - Morphine
        - Amphetamines
        - Methamphetamines

- Schedule III
  - Potential for abuse (less potential than Schedule I or II)
  - Accepted medical use
  - Abuse of the drug may lead to moderate or low physical or psychological dependence
  - Substances are only available (legally) via prescription
  - Examples (not all inclusive) of Schedule III:
    - Barbiturate
    - Anabolic Steroids
    - Codeine
- Schedule IV
  - Potential for abuse is low
  - Widely accepted medical use
  - Abuse of the drug may lead to low physical or psychological dependence
  - Examples (not all inclusive) of Schedule IV:
    - Darvocet
    - Chloral hydrate (sleeping pills)
- Schedule V
  - Potential for abuse is low
  - Widely accepted medical use
  - Abuse of the drug may lead to limited physical or psychological dependence
  - Examples (not all inclusive) of Schedule V:
    - Cough suppressants with small amounts of codeine
    - Anti-diarrheas with small amounts of opium

This portion of the test will account for approximately eleven percent of the questions. Part III will cover:

- Nervous system
- Actions of drugs
- Drug interactions

## NERVOUS SYSTEM

The nervous system controls everything from breathing, thinking, feeling, and walking. It is comprised of the:

- Brain

- Spinal Cord

- All of the nerves in the body (the nerves act as messengers to the brain so the brain can respond to the stimuli)

The nervous system is a network of specialized cells (**neurons** and **glial cells**) that communicate information both within and outside the body, and it strives for stability (**homeostasis**). Therefore, the body is constantly responding to, and adjusting for: temperature, nutrients, metabolism, and organ function.

### MAJOR DIVISIONS OF THE NERVOUS SYSTEM

The nervous system is divided into two categories, the central nervous system (CNS), and the peripheral nervous system (PNS). The CNS is made up of the brain and spinal cord, while the PNS is made up of the sensory neurons found outside of the brain and spinal cord. The neurons between and within the systems create communication.

### *CENTRAL NERVOUS SYSTEM*

The central nervous system (CNS) is the largest part of the nervous system and includes the brain and spinal cord. The spinal cord is held and protected by the **spinal cavity**, the skull protects the brain, and the CNS is layered with a triple-tiered protective coat called the **meninges**.

The **reticular activating system** is the area in the brain that receives the sensory input and information from the **cerebral cortex** (found at the junction of the spine and brain). This part of the body is very susceptible to drug use, as it is responsible for the sleep/wake cycle.

## PERIPHERAL NERVOUS SYSTEM

The peripheral nervous system (PNS) is made up of the neurons that connect them to the CNS. The majority of the **axons** (called nerves) are in the PNS.

## PARTS OF THE NERVOUS SYSTEM

There are several parts of the nervous system that serve separate functions:

- Neurons
    - o Process and transmit information.
    - o Core component of the brain, spinal cord, and peripheral nerves.
    - o Different type of neurons exist:
        - **Sensory neurons** respond to touch, sound, light, and other stimuli.
        - **Motor neurons** receive signals from the brain that cause responses based on the stimuli.
- Glial Cells
    - o Non-neuron cells.
    - o Provide support and nutrition, and maintain homeostasis.
    - o Functions of the **glial cells** are:
        - Surround neurons, holding them in place.
        - Supply nutrients and oxygen to neurons.
        - Insulate neurons from each other.
        - Destroy pathogens and remove dead neurons.

## COMMUNICATIONS WITHIN THE NERVOUS SYSTEM

Neurons do not actually touch. There is a small gap between neurons called the **synaptic cleft**. The junction between the neurons is called the **synapse**. The communication that is carried by the neurons is done through an electric-like transmission (**nerve impulse**). The nerve impulse is relayed across the synaptic cleft from one nerve to the next.

### THE NERVES

The nervous system is made up of specialized nerve cells (**neurons**). Neurons are designed to send and receive messages through **neurotransmitters** (chemical messages released by neurons).

- The message is sent to the communication point (**synapse**).
- The neurons have tree-like branches (**dendrites**) that pick up communications.
- Depending on the message sent, the receiving neuron is either excited or inhibited.
    - If the message excites the neuron, then an electric-like communication travels to the receiving region (**axon**).

Neurotransmitters are affected by drugs to alter the synthesis, storage, release, or deactivate. The main neurotransmitters found in the nervous systems are:

- **Acetylcholine** (ACh)
    - Found in the brain and is responsible largely for the autonomic portion of the PNS.
- **Catecholamine**
    - Fight or flight hormones that have similar chemical structure to norepinephrine and epinephrine.
    - **Dopamine**
        - Elevates mood and psychotic behavior.
        - Controls fine muscle movement and endocrine functions.
- **Serotonin**
    - Controls appetite and mood.

ACTIONS OF DRUGS

There are several factors that influence the actions of drugs.

- **Main effects** are the intended drug response.
- **Side effects** are the unintended drug response. Common side effects are:
  - Vomiting and nausea
  - Changes in mental alertness
  - Allergic reaction
    - Body tries to destroy the drug through rashes, hives, itching, shock, or respiratory difficulty.
  - Dependence to avoid withdrawal
  - Cardiovascular changes
- **Tolerance** (body's decreased response with the same dosage)
  - Develops at varying levels depending on the drug and the person's sensitivity to it.
  - **Reverse-tolerance (sensitization)** sometimes happens when a body develops a greater response to a lesser dose.
  - **Cross-tolerance** is the development of tolerance to drugs in the same "family" as another.
- **Potency** (amount of drug necessary to cause effect)
- **Toxicity** (capacity of drug to do damage)
- **Time** response factors
  - **Acute** – immediate.
  - **Chronic** – long term.
  - **Cumulative** – build-up of a drug in the body after multiple doses in short intervals.

Factors that influence the effect of drugs are:

- **Administration**
  - How is the drug introduced into the body?

- **Absorption**
  - How does the drug move from administration to the system it is supposed to affect?
- **Distribution**
  - How does the drug move to various areas in the body?
- **Activation**
  - How is the drug used to produce an effect?
- **Elimination**
  - How is the drug metabolized out of the body?
  - **Biotransformation**
    - Process of changing chemical properties of a drug (typically done by the liver).
  - **Half-life**
    - Time needed for the body to eliminate half-dose of the drug.
- **Physiological variables**
  - Age
    - Young and old need fewer drugs to achieve effect.
  - Gender
    - Body size, composition, and hormones affect drug's influence.
    - Pregnant women should watch out for **teratogenic** (physical harm to fetus) effects.

## ADMINISTRATION OF DRUGS

There are several methods to ingest drugs that vary depending on the type of drug and desired effect.

- Ingestion
  - o Drug enters through wall of stomach or intestine.
  - o Least effective and most convenient method.
- Inhalation
  - o Enters through the lungs, which use the capillaries to cross membranes.
  - o Rapid reaction.
- Injection
  - o Intravenous (in vein).
    - ▪ Fastest method for drug reaction; less drug is needed for reaction.
  - o Intramuscular (in muscle).
  - o Subcutaneous (beneath skin).
- Topical application
  - o Drug passes through skin.

## DRUG INTERACTIONS

There are three possible effects from combining drug use. The three effects of combining drugs are:

- **Additive**
  - o Drugs combine in the system, but they do not exaggerate one another.
- **Antagonistic**
  - o Drug cancels the effect of another.
- **Potentiated**
  - o One drug actually intensifies the effect of another.
  - o The potentiated effects of drugs have caused many unplanned emergencies and deaths.

PART IV. ALCOHOL

This portion of the test will account for approximately twelve percent of the questions. Part IV will cover:

- History and types
- Determinants of blood alcohol level
- Effects
- Uses and Administration
- Tolerance, withdrawal, and overdose
- Dependency issues
- Prevention and treatment

## HISTORY AND TYPES

This section covers a brief history of alcohol, how alcohol is made (and the types), and the general public's attitudes toward alcohol.

### ALCOHOL HISTORY

Alcohol is second only to caffeine in use. The largest New England commodity was rum in the triangle trade. The heaviest drinking period in the United States was when Jefferson was president (1801-1809). Over one hundred years later (1919) the Eighteenth Amendment was passed to ban alcohol (**Prohibition**). The effect was not what the government intended, as criminal activity soared. From **bootlegging** (selling homemade illegal alcohol through underground channels) to "speakeasies" there was a general disregard for the law. In 1933, the Twenty-First Amendment was passed to repeal Prohibition.

### HOW ALCOHOL IS MADE

Alcohol is created from the fermentation process of grains or fruit. The first alcoholic beverage was probably **mead** (made from fermented honey). The **fermentation** produces ethanol or ethyl alcohol when the yeast converts the sugars. Fermentation will continue until all of the sugar has been consumed and the alcohol has reached a concentration that kills the yeast (12-14%).

Greater alcohol content can be achieved through **distillation**. The Arabs developed distilling in 800 A.D. by boiling the fermented drinks, recapturing the vapor, and increasing the concentration of alcohol by 50%. The **still** made the process of getting drunk easier for people, and alcohol abuse increased. **Proof** is the measurement of how much alcohol is in a drink. Proof is expressed as twice of the total amount of a beverage. Proof is typically a measurement for liquors. For example, an eighty-proof bottle of whiskey is forty percent alcohol. Typical proofs are as follows:

- United States beers 4-6%
- Wine coolers 10-12%
- Dessert wines 17-20%
- Liquors 22-50%
- Distilled spirits 40-50%

Ethyl alcohol is the alcohol used for consumption; however, there are other types of alcohol as well:

- Methyl alcohol
  - Made from wood
  - Is poison to consume
  - Added to ethyl alcohol for industrial items so the industrial items are not abused
- Ethylene glycol
  - Used in antifreeze
- Isopropyl alcohol
  - Antiseptic
  - Rubbing alcohol

### ATTITUDES ABOUT ALCOHOL

Alcohol is seen as a social lubricant. There is a general belief that drinking is safe, promotes social interaction, and makes someone more extroverted. People are under the general impression that alcohol is relatively harmless because:

- It is legal
- Advertisements abound
- Media promotes its use

### DETERMINANTS OF BLOOD ALCOHOL LEVEL

The factors that relate to the rate of alcohol absorption are:
- Strength of alcohol
- Number of drinks
- How closely the drinks are consumed

- Emptiness of the stomach
  - Fatty foods (meat, milk) slow the absorption
  - Diluting with water can slow the absorption
  - Mixing with carbonated drinks increases absorption by causing the stomach to empty into the small intestine more rapidly
- Size of the person
- Gender
  - Since women have a higher percentage of body fat the **blood alcohol concentration** (BAC) is usually higher for the same amount of alcohol consumed by a man.

Once the alcohol is in the blood it is evenly distributed to all tissues (including fetal circulation during pregnancy). Since the brain uses a lot of blood the intoxication is felt quickly.

Alcohol has almost no vitamins, minerals, or dietary needs. Empty calories derived from carbohydrates make up alcohol. The principle enzyme that metabolizes alcohol is the **alcohol dehydrogenase**, which is found mostly in the liver. The blood alcohol concentration (BAC) rises when the liver cannot oxidize it.

EFFECTS

It is common to take alcohol with other drugs to intensify their effects. Short-term effects are similar to sedative hypnotics, such as:

- Disinhibition
- Euphoria
- Friendliness
- Aggression
- Hostility

Alcohol leads people to misinterpret sexual signals and can lead to:

- Unwanted sexual behaviors
- Acquaintance or date rape
- Unplanned pregnancy
- Sexually transmitted disease

EFFECTS ON THE BODY

Alcohol depresses the central nervous system and influences all major organs, causing physical and behavioral dependence. The liver is responsible for removing approximately 95% of alcohol in the bloodstream. Therefore, once the liver cannot keep up with the consumption, the alcohol level in the bloodstream rises. Alcohol has a significant effect on nearly every major organ in the body:

- Brain
  - Depresses cerebellum
    - Slurred speech
    - Staggering
  - Depresses respiratory system
    - Can result in death
  - Impairs production of dopamine and serotonin
  - Mental functions impaired
- Liver
  - Most common cause of alcoholic-related death
  - Alcoholic fatty liver
    - First stage

- Liver increases production of fat, enlarging the liver (**hepatotoxic effect**)
- Reversible if user abstains
    - Second stage
        - Fat cells multiply and swelling causes alcoholic hepatitis
        - Chronic inflammation can be fatal
        - Reversible if user abstains
    - Third and final stage
        - Scars form on liver and liver becomes fibrous and hard
        - Good tissue deteriorates, causing **cirrhosis** (sir-RO-sis)
        - Leading cause of death among alcoholics
        - 15% of alcoholics have this, and the effects are not reversible
- Digestive system
    - Damages tissue
        - Acid imbalance
        - Inflammation
        - Acute gastric distress (**gastritis**)
        - Heartburn
    - Cancer of the mouth and esophagus chances double
    - Ulcers, hernias, and cancers in the digestive track
    - If combined with smoking the odds of cancer are 15 times greater
    - Damage to pancreas can cause alcoholic diabetes
- Blood
    - Production of red, white, and platelets decreases.
    - Problems clotting
    - More susceptible to infection
    - Lower resistance to disease
    - **Anemia** (low iron in the blood)

- Cardiovascular system
  - Dilation of blood vessels in skin
  - Flushing, warmth in skin
  - Heart composition change to fat and fiber (**alcoholic cardiomyopathy**)
    - Irregular heartbeat, arrhythmia, high blood pressure, strokes
  - However, two drinks or less of wine per day can reduce incidence of heart disease, heart attacks, strokes, and high blood pressure
- Sexual organs
  - Men
    - Inflames prostate
    - Lowers sperm count
    - Impotence
    - Loss of body hair
    - Infertility
  - Women
    - Menstrual delays
    - Ovary abnormality
    - Infertility
- Endocrine system
  - Affects hypothalamus, pituitary glands, and gonads
  - Testosterone decreases
- Kidney
  - Damage to kidneys, causing metabolic complications
  - Urinary tract infections common
- Brain
  - Affects memory, judgment, and learning ability
  - Wernicke-Korsakoff syndrome
    - Psychotic condition caused by alcohol (nutritional and vitamin deficiency)
    - Inability to remember recent events and compensate by making up fictional ones
- Fetus
  - Alcohol crosses placenta
  - The fetus cannot oxidize alcohol properly

- o Can cause spontaneous abortion
- o **Fetal alcohol syndrome** (FAS)
  - Facial deformities
  - Low birth weight
  - Stunted growth
  - Mental retardation
    - Mild to moderate permanent retardation
  - Learning disabilities
  - Joint problems
  - Physical characteristics
    - A small head with widely set eyes
  - The more the mother drinks the more severe the damage
- o Joint and limb deformities
- o Birth weight low
- Malnutrition
  - o The empty calories from alcohol make the person less hungry for actual nutrients

EFFECTS OF QUANTITIES OF ALCOHOL

Moderate quantities of alcohol:
- Increases the heart rate
- Dilates the blood vessels
- Lowers blood pressure
- Stimulates appetite
- Stimulates urine production
- Increases drowsiness
- Incapacitates individual's ability to think and talk

Larger quantities of alcohol cause:
- Significant confusion and coordination issues
- Disorientation
- Anesthesia
- Coma
- Death

The Blood Alcohol Concentration (BAC) graph below indicates specific symptoms prevalent according to a person's BAC. Typically a person passes out before they drink enough to die. As a rule it typically takes as many hours as drinks to sober up:

| BAC level | Behaviors |
|---|---|
| .05% (1/2 part alcohol to every 1000 part blood) | Inhibitions are less stringent, and the everyday worries of life are released ("buzzed") |
| .1% (1 part alcohol to every 1000 part blood) | May not feel intoxicated, but the individual loses some coordination (most states consider this legally intoxicated) |
| .2% (2 part alcohol to every 1000 part blood) | This is the obnoxious drunk at the party; may be boisterous, loud, aggressive, and staggering |
| .3% (3 part alcohol to every 1000 part blood) | Comprehension is severely compromised; person will likely be unable to communicate coherent thoughts |
| .4-.5% (4-5 part alcohol to every 1000 part blood) | DANGER! Risk of fatal intoxication (alcohol poisoning); Central Nervous System begins to shut down and brain activity slows |

Alcohol is also commonly known as "liquid courage" or "social lubricant" because its intoxicating ingredients make people more outgoing, relaxed, adventuresome, and forgetful of their inhibitions. While some people think that alcohol is a stimulant, it is actually a depressant. Because alcohol is transmitted via the bloodstream it influences nearly every organ in the body. There are several types of alcoholics:

- Alpha alcoholic
    - Psychological dependence to cope
    - Irritable and anxious when not drinking
- Beta Alcoholic
    - Social dependence
    - Consumes to meet social obligation
- Gamma alcoholic
    - Loss of control when alcohol is consumed
- Delta alcoholic
    - Maintenance drinker
        - Cannot abstain for a day or two
        - Common in wine-drinking countries
            - Sip wine most waking hours
            - Tipsy but atypical to be inebriated
- Epsilon alcoholic
    - Binge drinker
        - Excess drinking for a period, then abstains until next binge
- Zeta alcoholic
    - May or may not be addicted, but becomes violent when drunk

**Problem drinking** is when someone doesn't need drinks to support body functions (they aren't psychologically or physically dependent), but when they do drink they cause problems for themselves or others.

## TOLERANCE, WITHDRAWAL, AND OVERDOSE

Alcoholism is a complex disease; it has both psychological and physical symptoms.

### TOLERANCE

Tolerance happens quickly with alcohol. Consequently, consumption increases to achieve the same effects. The increase in consumption can lead to severe physical and psychological dependence. Chronic abusers learn to compensate for their inebriation by modifying their behavior (**behavioral tolerance**).

### WITHDRAWAL

Alcoholics must drink for their body to operate normally. Alcohol withdrawals include shaking, nausea, vomiting, occasionally hallucinations, shock, and cardiac arrest. An occasional withdrawal symptom is hallucinations paired with shaking (the scientific name for this condition is **delirium tremens**, or DTs).

If the alcoholic is in otherwise good physical condition they can typically get through treatment via an outpatient program. Symptoms will begin to appear within 12-72 hours and include:

- Severe muscle tremors
- Nausea
- Anxiety
- Delirium Tremens

Between 24-48 hours the withdrawal symptoms for alcohol peak.

### OVERDOSE

The most common sign of over-consumption of alcohol is the hangover. A hangover can consist of:

- Upset stomach
- Nausea
- Headache
- Sensitivity to sounds
- Ill temper

Whiskey, scotch, and rum hangovers appear to be worse than vodka and gin (possibly because there are fewer impurities in the latter). There are different ineffective treatments for a hangover including:

- Taking a drink of the same beverage in the morning ("taking the hair of the dog that bit you")
    - Can increase physical dependency on alcohol
- Taking aspirin and caffeine before drinking to control the morning headache, and counteract the depressant effects of alcohol
    - Not proven to help, and the aspirin can cause irritation in the stomach, making a hangover worse.

However, much more serious than a hangover is the possibility of alcohol poisoning. **Alcohol poisoning** (acute alcohol intoxication) is a potentially fatal condition that is caused by the rapid increase in the BAC level due to consumption of alcoholic beverages. The symptoms of alcohol poisoning are:

- Unconsciousness
- Weak and rapid pulse (>100 beats per minute)
- Clammy skin
- Bluish hue to the skin (for darker pigments the nail beds will be an indication of the blue tint)

Any person suffering from alcohol poisoning will need immediate medical attention. Watch the victim to ensure they are safe (as you wait for medical help to arrive); a complication of alcohol poisoning is asphyxiation (lack of oxygen to the brain) by choking on their own vomit.

## DEPENDENCY ISSUES

Dependency issues exist for both the alcoholic and the loved ones around them. Much of the dependency on alcohol depends on:

- **Denial**
    - o When an alcoholic cannot admit that they have a problem.
- **Enabling**
    - o Loved ones' refusal to admit drinking is a problem.

## DEPENDENCY WITHIN THE ALCOHOLIC

Dependency can range from mild psychological dependence to the more serious physical dependence. Physical dependence on alcohol is exhibited through various symptoms in alcohol's absence:

- Anxiety
- Agitation
- Confusion
- Insomnia
- Delirium Tremens
- Convulsions
- Death

The extended use of large quantities of alcohol is associated with irreversible brain damage and/or dementia.

## DEPENDENCY WITHIN THE FAMILY

Alcoholism is a serious issue and has lasting impacts on the alcoholic and those around them. Children and spouses of alcoholics are typically labeled as **co-dependents** of alcohol. The alcoholic is depending on alcohol to function, and the children and spouse depend on the alcoholic. Therefore, the spouse and children also depend on the alcohol.

## *CHILDREN OF ALCOHOLICS*

Adult Children of Alcoholics (ACOA) exhibit similar traits across personality types. While not always the case, ACOAs typically:

- Take themselves too seriously

- Overreact to changes
- Have problems following through on a project
- Judge themselves mercilessly
- Have a high risk of becoming alcoholic
- Are more likely to marry an alcoholic
- Suffer from depression and anxiety

Small children suffer from more sleep issues, including:
- Crying
- Bed wetting
- Nightmares

Teens exhibit specific symptoms, including:
- Perfectionism
- Hoarding
- Loners
- Self-consciousness
- Phobias

The top ten roles that children play in the life of an alcoholic are:
- The family hero
- Scapegoat
- Lost child
- Mascot
- Placater
- Hypochondriac
- Pseudo parent to younger children
- Pseudo parent to alcoholic
- Pseudo spouse to sober parent
- Refuge for younger children

### SPOUSES OF ALCOHOLICS

Typically spouses become **enablers** by making excuses for the addict. The top ten roles that a spouse plays in the life of an alcoholic are:
- Rescuer
- Martyr
- Blamer
- Fellow drinker
- Placater
- Super responsible

- Super composed
- Hypochondriac
- Scapegoat
- Avoider

## *ALCOHOLIC DEMOGRAPHICS*

Women make up one-quarter of the alcoholic population.
They tend to fit some of the following categories:
- Drink alone
- Unemployed and looking for work
- Divorced, separated, or single
- Unmarried but living with a man
- In twenties or early thirties
- Have heavy-drinking husbands or partners
- Have masculine roles (blue-collar or female executives)
- Were physically or sexually abused as children

Women develop cirrhosis faster than men and suffer from domestic violence 15 times more often when spouses drink.

The demographics for alcohol use are as follows:
- Caucasians have the highest alcohol use, followed by Hispanics, then African Americans.
- The higher the education the more likely alcohol is used.

Alcohol use is worldwide, but treated very differently across cultures:
- Italians use wine as if it were a food.
- Orthodox Jews use wine for spiritual purposes.
- Finnish, Polish, and Russian cultures are associated with binge drinking.
- French are associated with sipping throughout the day.
- The United States ranges among all of the activities.

Alcohol abuse is responsible:

- For at least 100 billion dollars when considering:
  o Insurance
  o Criminal justice
  o Treatment
  o Lost productivity
- Half of all highway accidents are attributed to alcohol use.

With the statistics and facts indicating the dangers of alcohol, why is it still in use?

- America finds alcohol to be sexy and sophisticated.
- Impulsive behaviors are encouraged.
- The drinker can, and is expected to, engage in non-customary behavior.

There are also social issues directly related to alcohol abuse. A direct correlation between accidents, crime and violence, suicide, and alcohol can be drawn.

There are several organizations that are related to curbing alcohol abuse.

- **Alcoholics Anonymous (AA)**
- **Mothers Against Drunk Driving (MADD***)* is** another group focused on alcohol reduction, which was founded by Candy Lightner after her daughter was killed in 1980.
- **Students Against Drunk Driving (SADD)**, which is a group that focuses on high school students that enforces a contractual agreement between parent and child.

## *TREATMENT FOR ALCOHOLISM*

There are several treatment options for alcoholics with varying levels of success. Ultimately, the user must want to stop for any one treatment to assist them in their goal. Some of the treatment options are:

- Alcoholics Anonymous (AA)
    - o The level of success and amount of members are hard to assess because the membership is voluntary and anonymous.
    - o The tendency of the people that participate in AA are:
        - ▪ Middle-class
        - ▪ Socially conservative
        - ▪ Not hard-core alcoholics
    - o There are two types of meetings:
        - ▪ Open
            - • Anyone with an interest can attend
            - • Approximately 45 minutes

- Closed
  - Those that have shown only a serious desire to stop alcohol use are invited to attend.
- The key to AA is the twelve-step program that is rooted in a belief in God. The twelve steps are:
  - Admit powerlessness over alcohol
  - Power greater than self can restore them
  - Give life to God
  - Reinvent self morally
  - Admit to God, self, and others their moral indiscretions
  - Ask God to remove character defects
  - Humbly ask God to forgive
  - List all people harmed and try to make amends
  - Continue to admit when wrong
  - Pray for God's will
  - Spread message to other alcoholics
- Rehabilitation facilities
  - Minnesota Model
    - One month in an inpatient situation with a formal treatment plan.
    - Once the alcohol is out of the system and the acute stages of withdrawal have passed, they may be given long-term sedatives (Valium or Librium).
    - Typically a prescription for disulfiram (Antabuse) is offered.
      - **Antabuse** is a drug that blocks the metabolism of alcohol, and any alcohol will cause very unpleasant symptoms (headache, flushing, and nausea).

- - A patient has to decide two days before drinking to stop Antabuse.
  - o Intensive outpatient rehab
    - ▪ 15-30 hours within a facility
  - o Halfway houses
    - ▪ Residential environment where people are in the program and looking for work (or are working).
  - o Long term care facilities
    - ▪ Residential settings where people are not ready to integrate back into society (work, etc.).
- Detoxification units
  - o Three to seven days in length; the patient may actually go through this many times. It is not proven to have a long-term effect to abstain from alcohol.
- Therapeutic communities
  - o Counseling and other activities that advocate lifestyle changes.

## *ALCOHOLICS STATISTICS*

There are many facts that make alcoholism very difficult to treat including:

- Because of the legality of alcohol it is easier to be in denial of a problem.
- Alcoholics are more likely to relapse (because of the social acceptance of alcohol).
- Alcoholics are emotionally fragile.
- Acute alcoholic withdrawal syndrome is intense and painful.

## Part V. Anti-anxiety and Sedative Hypnotics

This test is divided among many areas of substance abuse. This portion of the test will account for approximately six percent of the questions. Part V will cover:

- History and types
- Effects
- Uses and administration
- Tolerance, withdrawal, and overdose
- Prevention and treatment
- Dependency issues

## History and Types

The anti-anxiety and sedative hypnotics are the most widely used and abused drugs in the United States. They are used to relieve stress and induce sleep.

### History

Sedatives were discovered based on a need to find CNS depressants that were not alcohol. Some of the main users of CNS depressants were homemakers.

- Bromides
  - Used in the early 1900s
- Barbiturates
  - Replaced bromides
  - Found to cause dependence and lethal overdose
- Benzodiazepines
  - Replaced barbiturates in the 1950s
  - Safe for short periods
  - Long-term use can cause dependence and withdrawal

### Types

The major types of anti-anxiety and sedative hypnotics are:

- Benzodiazepines
  - Varying effects such as anti-anxiety, insomnia treatment, anti-convulsion, muscle relaxant, and sleep induction

- o CNS depressant
- o Librium (chlordiazepoxide) and Valium (diazepam) are commonly prescribed benzodiazepines
- Barbiturates
  - o Risk of abuse and addiction is high
  - o Mostly considered obsolete for treating anxiety
  - o When used as a hypnotic it causes an unnatural sleep, which makes the user feel unsatisfied with sleep
  - o Largely replaced by benzodiazepines (considered less dangerous)
  - o Methaqualone Quaalude ("ludes"), and Sopor are common barbiturates
- Solvent sedatives
  - o Ether
  - o Ethyl alcohol (alcoholic beverage)
  - o Chloroform
- Non-benzodiazepines sedatives
  - o Lunesta
- Uncategorized sedatives
  - o Gamma-hydroxybutyrate (GHB)

EFFECTS

The effects of hypnotics vary widely on the dosage. Ranging from a mild depression of the CNS to anesthesia. Some of the effects of barbiturates include:

- Respiratory depression
- Lowered blood pressure
- Fatigue
- Euphoria
- Relaxed contentment

Some of the side effects include:

- Drowsiness
- Light-headedness
- Lethargy
- Rashes
- Nausea
- Diminished libido
- Increased sensitivity to alcohol
- Irregular menstruation

## USES AND ADMINISTRATION

Abusers and the medical community use and administer anti-anxiety and sedative hypnotics.

### USES

The medical uses of anti-anxiety and sedative hypnotics are:

- Anxiety relief
- Treatment of neurosis
- Muscle relaxation
- Alleviate lower back pain
- Treat convulsive disorders
- Induce sleep
- Relieve withdrawal
- Induce amnesia (surgery or medical procedures)

Drug users prefer the short and intermediate acting barbiturates usually prescribed as sedative or sleeping pills. Short-term barbiturates' effects start within fifteen to forty minutes and last five to six hours.

### ADMINISTRATION

Sedative hypnotics are given a variety of ways including:

- Intravenously
- Intramuscularly
- Rectally
- Orally

## TOLERANCE, WITHDRAWAL, AND OVERDOSE

Frequent use of anti-anxiety and sedative hypnotics can cause tolerance, physical dependence, and psychological dependence.

### TOLERANCE

Tolerance to barbiturates occurs more often than with benzodiazepines (which are considered safer). Tolerance is one of the reasons that barbiturates have limited use in medicine today. However, benzodiazepines also develop tolerance and physical dependence in as little as two months of regular use.

### WITHDRAWAL

Withdrawal can be a long process (up to a year). Symptoms include:

- Anxiety
- Irritability
- Sweating
- Tremors
- Sleep disorders
- Depersonalization
- Hypersensitivity to stimuli
- Depression
- Psychosis

### OVERDOSE

Symptoms of an overdose are:

- Sluggishness
- Lack of coordination
- Difficulty thinking
- Impaired speech
- Impaired judgment
- Coma
- Shallow breathing

The lethal dose varies greatly based on individual and tolerance. Overdose is much more likely and deadly if the drugs are paired with other CNS depressants such as alcohol.

If the drugs are needed medically they should be taken in the dosages prescribed and for as little time as possible. Because abrupt withdrawal can be hazardous a gradual medically supervised withdrawal is recommended.

## DEPENDENCY ISSUES

Low doses relieve tension; however, anti-anxiety medications carry risks such as:

- Lack of safety
- Tendency for tolerance
- Dependence
- Withdrawal symptoms
- Potential for abuse
- Common drug interactions

Dependency has several symptoms/characteristics such as:

- Having taken the drugs for four months or longer
- Reliance on drugs to cope (psychological dependence)
- Anxiety and/or sleeplessness returns at reduced or no dose
- Less effect on same dosage (tolerance)
- Increased dose when stressed
- Increased alcohol intake

## PART VI. INHALED SUBSTANCES

This portion of the test will account for approximately four percent of the questions. Part VI will cover:

- History and types
- Effects
- Uses and administration
- Tolerance, withdrawal, and overdose
- Prevention and treatment
- Dependency issues

### HISTORY AND TYPES

**Inhalants** are volatile drugs that produce drunk-like effects very quickly and cheaply.

#### HISTORY

Some of the popular inhalants (chloroform, diethyl ether, and nitrous oxide) were first used in medicine. The "father" of nitrous oxide abuse is Sir Humphrey Davy, who held nitrous oxide parties.

#### TYPES

Common household items can be inhaled (gasoline, paint, paint thinner). Unfortunately, the results can be fatal. There are three types of inhalants:

- Volatile solvents
  - Glue
  - Paint thinner
  - Aerosols from paints
  - Hairspray
  - Cookware coating agents
  - Liquid paper correction
  - Nail polish remover
  - Felt tip marking pens
  - Gasoline and lighter fluid
- Anesthetics
  - **Nitrous oxide** (laughing gas) is the most common.
  - **Chloroform** initially used for anesthetic, but has largely been replaced.

- Nitrites
  - Abused by a few select groups.
  - Use declined in 1991 after the chemicals were banned.

## EFFECTS

The effects range from mild relaxation to death.

### LOW DOSES

- Brief feeling of light-headedness
- Loss of control
- Lack of coordination
- Disorientation
- Dizziness
- Possible hallucinations

### HIGH DOSES

- Relaxation
- Depression leading to sleep or a coma
- Hypoxia (lack of oxygen causing brain damage or death)
- Motor impairment
- Psychological problems
- Lung, kidney, liver, airway damage (some irreversible)

### USES AND ADMINISTRATION

Inhalants range from household products to legitimate drugs used in the medical arena. Upon inhalation of the solvent or gas the lungs rapidly absorb and distribute the substance through capillaries. Users inhale the vapors using plastic bags held over their mouths, or by breathing solvents from a soaked rag or container. Young people (ages 12-17) have the highest rate of abuse of inhalants. Inhalants are used most commonly by young people because they are:

- Easy to hide
- Inexpensive
- Accessible
- Uninformed on the dangers of inhalants

Nitrous oxide is abused usually in the medical community (largely due to the accessibility of the substance).

TOLERANCE, WITHDRAWAL, AND OVERDOSE

Inhalants are dangerous for several reasons:

- The solvent or chemical may be toxic
- Behavior while intoxicated
- **Hypoxia** (lack of oxygen)
- Pneumonia
- Cardiac arrest
- Brain damage
  - o Typically from long-term chronic use

Typically death by overdose is caused by a very high concentration of the chemical (e.g., inhaling from a plastic bag or in a closed area). The most common cause of death from solvent abuse is from vomiting while unconscious (**aspiration**).


PREVENTION AND TREATMENT

Inform children on the danger of inhalants and keep a close eye for symptoms and signs of abuse.


DEPENDENCY ISSUES

Typically inhalants are abused by a select group of people.

- Younger kids
- Socioeconomically depressed areas
- People that don't have access to other drugs
  - o Incarcerated people
  - o Institutionalized people

It appears to be a "faddish" drug where people mature out of using them.

## PART VII. TOBACCO AND NICOTINE

This portion of the test will account for approximately seven percent of the questions. Part VII will cover:

- History and types
- Effects
- Uses and administration
- Tolerance, withdrawal, and overdose
- Prevention and treatment
- Dependency issues

### HISTORY AND TYPES

It is currently the sixth largest legal crop in the United States (North Carolina and Kentucky are the leading growers).

#### HISTORY

Tobacco began in the United States as a popular export of Virginia. A brief timeline of the important parts of the tobacco industry are:

- 1870s
    - Cigarette girls rolled about four cigarettes in a minute.
- 1883
    - James Duke leased and improved the first cigarette-rolling machine that could make 200 cigarettes in a minute (today the cigarette machines make 3,600 in a minute).
- 1964
    - U.S. Surgeon General reported the cigarette is related to lung cancer in men.
- 1965
    - Congress passed legislation for National Clearing House for Smoking and Health (responsible for monitoring and reviewing medical literature related to smoking and health).

- 1970
    - All cigarette packages had to read: "Warning: The Surgeon General Has Determined that Cigarette Smoking is Dangerous to Your Health."
- 1971
    - Congress banned advertising tobacco on radio and TV.
    - Tobacco industry suffered enormously.
- 1984
    - Congress required cigarette packs and print ads to post four distinct warnings that are rotated every three months.

## TYPES

There are over 60 species of tobacco. The nicotine potency ranges from .3-7% depending on the leaf position and the growing conditions. After the leaves are harvested they are:

- Dried
- Shredded
- Blown clean
- Moisturized with glycerin and other chemicals
- Packed in wooden barrels (**hogsheads**)

The FDA does not control the additives in tobacco products. Over 90% of the cigarettes sold in the United States have filter tips, which help remove some of the additives.

### THE COMPOUNDS OF THE CIGARETTE

The two phases of cigarettes are particulate and gaseous.
- The **particulate** phase is composed of the particles of the cigarette: nicotine, water, and the chemical compounds (tar).
- The **gaseous** phase is basically the smoke (carbon monoxide).

One in four regular smokers will die from tobacco use. Smoking affects almost every system within the body.

### PHYSIOLOGICAL EFFECTS OF TOBACCO

**Nicotine** (the addictive ingredient in tobacco) stimulates neurotransmitters to create arousal feelings. However, in larger doses the central nervous system begins to slow, creating feelings of relaxation. Some of the effects of smoking are:

- Salivary stimulation
- Hunger inhibition
- Deadens the taste buds
- Breathlessness

The physiological effects of tobacco vary based on the following:

- How densely the cigarette is packed
- Cigarette length
- Filter
- Volume of smoke inhaled
- Number of cigarettes in a day

### HEALTH EFFECTS OF TOBACCO USE

While it may soon be overcome by obesity, by the publishing date of this book smoking was the NUMBER ONE cause of premature deaths in the United States (19% of preventable deaths in the United States).

- The carbon monoxide that smoking generates combines with red blood cells in a process called **carboxyhemoglobin.**
  - The blood cell is unable to move oxygen through the system.
  - This condition is irreversible for red blood cells, and they are useless for the entirety of their lifecycle (120 days).
  - This condition also causes clotting problems.
  - Up to 10% of a smoker's blood can be in the form of carboxyhemoglobin.
- **COLD *(Chronic Obstructive Lung Disease)***
  - Inflammation or infection of the small airways that go into the lungs.

- **Pulmonary emphysema**
  - o Non-curable disease that destroys the **alveoli** (sacs where the air is transferred into the blood).
  - o Those that suffer pulmonary emphysema are almost always elderly people that have spent many years smoking.
- Reproduction difficulties
  - o Low sperm motility
  - o Lower hormone levels in women
  - o The carboxyhemoglobin suffocates the fetus increasing the likelihood of:
    - ▪ Stillborns
    - ▪ Miscarriages
    - ▪ Lower birth rates
    - ▪ Sudden Infant Death Syndrome (SIDS)
  - o Smoking combined with oral contraception increases the likelihood of strokes and heart attack.
- Smokers "cough"
  - o The small hairs (called **cilia**) that line the nose and ears become clogged with cigarette particulates making them less effective at their jobs.
- **Leukoplakia**
  - o Development of white leathery patches on gums, tongue, and inside cheeks.
  - o This condition can be a serious sign of cancer (or totally benign).
- Increased health risks
  - o Those that smoke pipes, cigars, and chew have a greater chance of cancer in the mouth and throat areas.
  - o Smoking increases lung cancer, cardiovascular disease (myocardial infarction- heart attack), and respiratory ailments.
- Cancer
  - o Lung cancer is the leading cause of cancer death in the United States.

- 82% of men and 75% of women that have lung cancer were smokers.
- 85-90% of lung cancer deaths are a result of smoking.
- Risk of lung cancer is related to the amount of smoke, duration, age at onset, degree of inhalation, and cigarette content.
  - Oral issues
    - Cancers are common in cigar, pipe, and smokeless tobacco users.
    - Smokeless tobacco users can suffer tooth loss, decay, and gum inflammation.

## Uses and Administration

There are no medical administrations for tobacco use.
Tobacco users administer the drug in one of four ways:

- Smoking
    - Cigarettes
    - Pipes
    - Cigars
- Chewing
    - Chewing tobacco leaves causes absorption of nicotine through the mucus lining of the mouth.
- Dip (moist snuff, spit tobacco)
    - Placing a pinch of tobacco between the gums and around the cheek area and spitting the unwanted saliva.
- Snuff
    - The least common method of absorption, snuff is ground tobacco, which is inhaled through the nose. In the United States snuff is sometimes applied like dip.

## Tolerance, Withdrawal, and Overdose

It is nearly impossible to overdose on tobacco and nicotine because of the small quantities in a cigarette. However, tolerance to smoking develops quickly, causing the habit to form rapidly. The body gets rid of nicotine so quickly that withdrawal symptoms occur close together, causing the need for more tobacco/nicotine products.

### Withdrawal

Extreme discomfort and urges to smoke are caused by withdrawal. These urges can last a few days up to several months. Most people get frustrated with the withdrawal process and begin smoking again.

Mortality ratios decline the longer an ex-smoker abstains. However, tobacco is one of the most difficult habits to quit.

- 70% of tobacco users want to quit but have been unsuccessful
  - 85% of illicit drug users who want to quit do.
  - 63% of people who try to quit cigarettes actually succeed.
- 83% of tobacco users do so daily
  - 10% of illicit drug users use daily

## PREVENTION

There are four primary aspects that are prevalent in the tobacco control laws to prevent their use:

- The right to smoke-free indoor air
- Prevent youths' access to tobacco products
- Limit advertising tobacco products
- Licensing those that do sell tobacco products

## TREATMENT

Tobacco users find it easy to slip back into the habit of smoking. The urge to smoke is provoked by both internal and external triggers. There are some ways that smokers can successfully quit. In order to reduce the smoking triggers smokers can:

- Nibble vegetables and fruit
- Chew gum or spices
- Replace smoking with the nicotine patch or gum
- Use nicotine patches
  - 24-hour patch giving small doses of nicotine to help stop the desire to smoke
- Perform physical activity
- Spend time in places where smoking is not permitted
- Use mouthwash after meals
- Spend time with nonsmokers
- Get rid of smoking paraphernalia

The demographics of those that successfully quit are typically:

- Above poverty level
- Solid education level

- White men

Tobacco is hypothesized to be a gateway drug. It is believed that smoking sets up patterns for related behaviors. This hypothesis is supported by the fact that many drug users initially begin by using alcohol and tobacco.

All forms of tobacco are unhealthy and develop physical and emotional dependence. While most people become dependent on smoking, there are a few, called "**chippers**," that can smoke a couple of cigarettes a day without dependence. Nicotine in tobacco is the drug that causes dependence.

Twenty-nine percent of the population (12 and older) smokes for different reasons such as:

- Peer pressure
- Ability to control a situation
- Self-medicating
- Influenced by the media
- Social rewards
- Conditioned to do so after some activities
- Ritual behavior
- No performance impairments
- Habitual

Tobacco products sometimes still contaminate people that do not smoke cigarettes.

- **Mainstream smoke**
  - The person smoking the cigarette, cigar, or pipe through the mouthpiece.
- **Side stream smoke**
  - The smoke released into the air from the lit tobacco product.
- **Passive smoking**
  - Person that inhales tobacco smoke who is not a smoker (**secondhand smoke**).

The demographics on tobacco use are:

- Drinkers or illicit drug users are more likely to smoke.
- Ancestry does not seem to make a difference.
- Men smoke more than women.
- College graduates are less likely to smoke.
- Smokeless tobacco products are more prevalent in whites.

## Part VIII. Psychomotor Stimulants

This portion of the test will account for approximately nine percent of the questions. Part VIII will cover:

- History and types
- Effects
- Uses and Administration
- Tolerance, withdrawal, and overdose
- Prevention and treatment
- Dependency issues

### History and types

Psychomotor stimulants ("**uppers**") increase alertness, excitation, and euphoria. They are responsible for almost half of all drug-related deaths in the United States.

#### History

Illicit stimulants have a sordid and varied past that dates back over 5,000 years.

- Over 5,000 years ago
    - Chinese used the ephedra plant (Ephedra Vulgaris) producing ma huang.
- 2500 B.C.
    - South American Indians living in Andean mountains chewed coca leaves for slow sustained administration of cocaine.
- Over 2,000 years ago
    - Coca plant leaves chewed in South America.
- 1880s
    - Cocaine isolated in the coca plant.
        - Cocaine powder, freebase, and crack are one of the most popular illicit drugs in the United States.
    - Sigmund Freud thought cocaine was a miracle drug and encouraged its medical use.

- 1887
    - Amphetamine synthesized by Lazar Edeleanu in Germany.
- 1918
    - Methamphetamine synthesized from ephedrine by Akira Ogata.
- 1927
    - Gordon Alles tested amphetamine on himself (looking for an ephedrine replacement).
- 1940s
    - World War II amphetamines and methamphetamines were given to fight fatigue and increase alertness.
    - Homemakers used amphetamines for weight control and boredom.
- 1949
    - Amphetamines withdrawn from the market because of the abuse.
- 1971
    - Amphetamine becomes a Schedule II drug under the Controlled Substances Act.
- 1980s
    - Cocaine use glamorized by celebrities.

TYPES

There are many types of psychomotor stimulants, ranging from mild and legal to significantly dangerous.

- **Amphetamine**
    - Methamphetamine ("crank," "ice")
        - **Methamphetamine** is related to amphetamine; however, it is longer lasting and more toxic.
        - Speed (injectable methamphetamine) made from an easy recipe.

- White odorless bitter tasting powder.
- **Crystal meth** (ice) is the most dangerous methamphetamine. Within seven seconds of ingestion the effect is felt, and it lasts for several hours (basically until the user can no longer physically sustain the high). Chronic use of crystal meth causes weight loss, compromised immunity system, damages major organs (liver, lungs, and kidneys).
  - o Designer Amphetamines
    - Sometimes different from amphetamine by a single element.
    - Derivative of amphetamine or methamphetamine.
    - All designer drugs are Schedule I.
    - Examples:
      - **Methylenedioxymethamphetamine** (MDMA) (Ecstasy)
      - **Methylenedioxyamphetamine** (MDA)
- Minor stimulants
  - o Caffeine
    - Legal drug that causes mild alertness.
    - The most used stimulant in the world.
    - Most caffeine is consumed through coffee beans and tea plants.
      - Coffee is derived from beans of the coffee plant (cultivated mainly in South America and Africa).
    - Most of the caffeine consumed in the United States by children and teens is through soda.
  - o Nicotine
    - Addictive property in the cigarette.

- **Cocaine**
  - Most powerful illicit stimulant.
  - Comes from coca leaves in South America harvested two to three times a year and produced into paste.
  - When snorted it is called **coke**, and when smoked it is either **freebase** (use of powder cocaine chemically altered and smoked through a pipe) or **crack** (coke mixed with baking soda that dries into rocklike crystals inhaled through a pipe).
  - Cocaine is an expensive habit because the effects of the drug last only from 5-30 minutes. During the "high" there is a feeling of exhilaration.
  - Processed in labs to form pure white hydrochloride salt powder.
  - Typically cut (**adulterated**) with powdered sugar, talc, arsenic, methamphetamine, or lidocaine.
  - Street names include blow, snow, flake, C, coke, toot, white lady, girl, Cadillac, nose candy, gold dust, and star dust.

EFFECTS

Psychomotor stimulants produce the following (in varying degrees depending upon their strength and method of administration):

- Sense of euphoria
- Wakefulness
- Increased physical activity
- Decreased appetite
- Increased respiration
- Feelings of power
- Strength
- Enhanced motivation

However, there are some significant side effects that accompany the desired effects:

- **Athetosis** (jerkiness of limbs)
- Irritability
- Insomnia
- Confusion
- Anxiety
- Irregular heartbeat
- Chest pain
- Respiration difficulties
- Nausea
- Dry mouth
- Hot flashes
- Sweating
- Irreversible damage to blood vessels that cause strokes
- Increased fetal complications
- Pupil dilation

Prolonged use of the illicit stimulants cause:

- Weight loss
- Sores
- Ulcers that do not heal
- Liver disease
- Hypersensitivity
- Stroke
- Heart attack
- Kidney damage
- Seizures

The effects of cocaine and amphetamines are similar; however, cocaine is more intense and disperses more rapidly.

Women that use cocaine during pregnancy often give birth to babies that will have lifelong health and mental issues. Many of these children are placed in the welfare system with little chance of adoption.

Cocaine and methamphetamine have no approved medical use in the United States. However, amphetamines are used for a couple of rare disorders. Methamphetamine and cocaine are frequently abused and dangerous drugs.

### USE

Amphetamine family of drugs is used medically for different purposes including:

- Treatment of narcolepsy
- Treatment of Attention Deficit Disorder (ADD) in children
- Treatment of extreme obesity

### ADMINISTRATION

There are four routes of drug administration:

- Snorting
  - Cocaine users snort cocaine powder through the nose for quick absorption into the bloodstream.
  - Methamphetamine and amphetamines can be snorted.
- Smoking
  - Cocaine users sometimes solidify the substances into rocks ("crack") and heat them while inhaling the vapors. Crack is inexpensive freebased cocaine that is ready for smoking.
    - **Freebasing** reduces the impurities and is more powerful than normal cocaine.
    - Treated with a liquid base (sodium carbonate or ammonium hydroxide), then a solvent (petroleum or ethyl ether).
    - Onset is rapid and dramatic, but the depression is more severe.
    - Street terms: baseball, bumping, white tornado, World Series, and snow toke.
  - Methamphetamine and amphetamines can be smoked.

- Injecting

    o Cocaine users can inject cocaine into the bloodstream.

    o Methamphetamine and amphetamines can be injected.

- Oral

    o Primary administration of legitimate use of amphetamine.

    o Methamphetamine can be dissolved into liquid and ingested.

Specifically for cocaine the intensity and duration of the effects are largely dependent on the method of administration. Injection and smoking produce a faster high than snorting. However, the faster and more intense the high, the shorter it lasts. Snorting may provide a high for 15 to 30 minutes while smoking or injection may last only 5 to 10. Amphetamines are sometimes administered with other drugs because they can intensify, prolong, or alter the effects. People that are dependent on opiates sometimes use amphetamine or cocaine (**speedballs**) in conjunction.

## TOLERANCE, WITHDRAWAL, AND OVERDOSE

Illicit stimulants are potent and dangerous. Because tolerance builds rapidly and the purity of drugs is difficult to discern, potentially fatal overdoses are likely.

### TOLERANCE

Tolerance to stimulants varies widely between individuals, their use, size, setting, and gender.

### WITHDRAWAL

While withdrawal from the powerful stimulants is considered very uncomfortable and intense it typically is not life threatening. Withdrawal goes through three distinct stages:

- Crash (nine hours to four days after drug use)
  - Suicidal thoughts
  - Depression
  - Anorexia
  - Fatigue
  - Insomnia
- Withdrawal (one to ten weeks)
  - Mood swings
  - Craving
  - Drug seeking
- Extinction (indefinitely)
  - Normal pleasure
  - Triggers can cause craving

Withdrawal from caffeine can last for several days and includes:

- Headaches
- Fatigue
- Mood changes
- Muscle pain
- Mild flu like symptoms
- Nausea

### OVERDOSE

An overdose of caffeine can cause:

- Restlessness
- Excitement
- Insomnia
- Muscle twitching

- Rambling thoughts and speech
- Gastrointestinal issues

An overdose of amphetamine can cause:

- Restlessness
- Rapid breathing
- Confusion
- Hallucinations
- Panic
- Aggressiveness
- Gastrointestinal issues
- Irregular heartbeat
- Seizures

An overdose of cocaine can cause:

- Itching (cocaine bugs)
- Tachycardia
- Hallucinations
- Delusions
- Respiratory failure
- Stroke
- Heart failure
- Renal failure
- Cerebral Hemorrhage

Prevention includes not having access to the triggers that caused initial drug use and choosing different peer (non-user) groups.

Treatment of dependence is based on the individual and can include:

- Cognitive behavioral therapy
- Inpatient treatment
- Outpatient treatment
    - Preferred to inpatient if the person has supportive environment
- Therapeutic drug treatment
    - To help with withdrawal, crash, and cravings

The reasons people become dependent on stimulants are:

- Euphoric properties

- Ability to combat fatigue

- Weight control

## AMPHETAMINES

Someone who has patterns of high dose and use of amphetamines is frequently called a "**speed freak**" or "**tweaker**". Speed freaks or tweakers are unpopular with the user peer group. They have:

- Unpredictable behavior

- Aggression

- Likely to be involved in violent crime

Users may live together in small ghettos called "**flash houses**". Abusers may have patterns of high dose use of amphetamines that can last as long as 15 days. During these "**runs**" the user may:

- Be unable to sleep

- Feel happy, powerful, and confident all of the time

- Eat very little

- Accomplish highly ambitious tasks

The run finishes when the bad effects outweigh the pleasurable ones. However, when the run has finished the user may:

- Sleep for many days

- Awaken hungry and depressed

Sometimes to overcome the effects of coming down from a run the user will:

- Smoke ice or inject speed which will start a new cycle

- Use barbiturates, benzodiazepines, and opiate narcotics to ease the crash or terminate a bad run

## COCAINE

Cocaine users will **binge** (similar to the amphetamines user's run). Users will re-administer cocaine every 10-30 minutes until the drug is gone. Meanwhile they will experience various symptoms including:

- Teeth grinding
- Difficulty thinking
- Irritability
- Suspiciousness
- Rebound effects
    - Depression
    - Fatigue
    - Over eating
- Fear
- **"Cocaine bugs"**
    - If withdrawing from cocaine the users may feel like insects are crawling all over their body.

Crack use is most common with:

- African Americans
- Hispanics

The popularity of crack use went up with the increase of the AIDS scare. However, AIDS is still a real threat for crack users. Under the influence and in order to acquire crack many people will have unprotected sex.

### CAFFEINE

Caffeine dependence is minor compared to the more powerful stimulants in this category. People are generally dependent on caffeine because:

- Socially accepted
- Easy to acquire
- Lower effect than other stimulants

## PART IX. OPIOIDS

This portion of the test will account for approximately nine percent of the questions. Part IX will cover:

- History and types
- Effects
- Uses and administration
- Tolerance, withdrawal, and overdose
- Prevention and treatment
- Dependency issues

### HISTORY AND TYPES

Opioids (opiates) come in four different types:

- Natural – actually contained in the resin of the poppy.

  o Morphine

    ▪ Only 2 of the 120 poppy species produce morphine

    ▪ Tolerance develops quickly

    ▪ Used in hospitals as a pain reliever

      • Used moderate or intense pain

      • Most useful in chronic dull pain

    ▪ Can be injected

      • Under the skin

        o When injected under the skin the effects of heroin and morphine are nearly identical.

      • Into the muscle

      • Into the vein

- o Codeine
  - Converted from morphine
  - Most common narcotic prescribed
  - Moderate pain relief found in:
    - Aspirin
    - Acetaminophen
    - Robitussin AC
    - Can be taken orally or injected
- o Thebaine
  - Not currently used for medical purposes
  - Produces stimulant effects (while other derivatives produce depressant effects)
  - Converted into many medically valid compounds
- Semi-synthetic – created from the natural opioids.
  - o Hydrocodone
    - Semi-synthetic opiate derived from codeine and thebaine
    - Is one of the main ingredients in Vicodin (pain relief)
      - Also used as a strong cough suppressant
  - o Oxycodone
    - Synthesized from thebaine

- Main active ingredient in many oral pain relief medications
- Combined with common analgesics
  - Acetaminophen (Percocet)
  - Aspirin (Percodan)
  - Ibuprofen (Combunox)
- Diacetylmorphine (heroin)
  - Synthesized from morphine
  - Pure heroin is a white powder
  - Brown (Mexican) heroin is caused by the unsatisfactory processing of the morphine
  - Arrives about 95% pure, then usually cut with lactose to increase profits and give the drug more bulk
  - Since heroin has a bitter taste, sometimes it is cut with quinine to disguise that it has been cut
    - Quinine has strong side effects including:
      - Vascular damage
      - Depressed respiration
      - Coma
      - Death
- Nicomorphine, dipropanoylmorphine desomorphine, hydromorphone, oxymorphone, and ethylmorphine

- Analgesics
- Derivatives of morphine
- Cough suppressants

- Fully synthetic – not derived from opiates, but the make-up effects the opiate receptors in the body
  - Fentanyl
    - 200 times more potent than morphine
    - Used to treat moderate to severe pain or for general anesthesia
  - Pethidine (Demerol), propoxyphene (Darvon), and tramadol
    - Used for moderate to severe pain
    - 1/10 as powerful as morphine
  - Methadone (Dolophine) "**Dollies**"
    - Analgesic, antitussive, and anti-addictive
    - Treats opiate dependence (by easing withdrawal) because of its cross-tolerance and long duration
- Endogenous – produced naturally in the body
  - Endorphins
  - Enkephalins
  - Dynorphins
  - Endomorphins

Opium has a long and controversial history in the world; a brief outline of its major historical points includes:

- 3400 B.C.
    - Lower Mesopotamia cultivates the poppy and passes this knowledge on to the Sumerians, who pass it to the Assyrians, who pass it to the Egyptians.
- 1300 B.C.
    - Egyptians cultivate poppy fields and the opium trade includes the Mediterranean Sea into Greece, Carthage, and Europe.
- 400 A.D.
    - Opium is introduced to China through Arab traders.
- 1620s – 1670s
    - Opium is the main commodity between Britain and China.
- 1700
    - Dutch teach Chinese the art of smoking opium in a pipe.
- 1729
    - Yung Cheng, Chinese emperor, prohibits opium smoking or sales (except for medicine).
- 1799
    - Kia King, Chinese emperor, bans opium completely; trade and cultivation become illegal.

- 1803
    - Friedrich Sertürner of Germany discovers the active ingredient in opium and neutralizes it with ammonia (creating alkaloids – or morphine). Morphine was named for the Greek god of dreams.
    - Physicians believe that morphine is "God's own medicine" because it is reliable, long lasting, and safe.
- 1839
    - Lin Tse-Hsu, imperial Chinese commissioner, orders foreign traders to surrender their opium.
    - British send warships to coast of China, thus beginning first Opium War.
    - In 1841 the British are triumphant, and the Treaty of Nanking is made in 1842.
- 1843
    - Dr. Alexander Wood administers morphine by injection resulting in instantaneous results with thrice the potency.
    - Used in U.S. Civil War and many men returned addicted to morphine (became known as "soldier's disease" or "army's disease").
- 1856
    - Second Opium War between France and Britain against China.
    - China loses again and importation of opium is legal.
- 1890
    - U.S. Congress imposes opium and morphine tax.
- 1895
    - The Bayer Company creates and manufactures heroin (**diacetylmorphine**), which won't go on sale until 1898.
    - Heroin becomes marketed as a cure for morphine addicts and used as a cough suppressant.
    - Touted as a heroic drug.
- 1914
    - Harrison Narcotic Act regulates opium. Until then the average addict was:
        - White woman
        - Southern

- ▪ Functioned well in the role of wife and mother
- ▪ Ordered the product from Sears Roebuck
- 1970-76
  - ○ Most heroin reached the states through the Golden Triangle of Southeast Asia.
  - ○ U.S. purchased most of the legal opium crop from Turkey to stop its conversion to heroin and other drugs.

Opiates activate opiate receptors, which mimic **endorphins** (the body's natural euphoric hormones). The receptor is either activated (**agonistic**) or blocked (**antagonistic**). The effects of opiates many times are outweighed by the side effects of the drugs. However, the highly addictive properties and rapid building tolerance of opiates make the drug difficult to cease once started.

### PHARMACOLOGICAL EFFECTS

Opiates have three major functions:

- **Analgesics** (pain relief)
    - Opiates relieve pain by activating some of the endorphin receptors.
    - The endorphin receptors block the transmission of pain, and alter the brain perception of pain in the pain center.
    - Its effectiveness lies in the fact that the narcotics do both.
- **Antitussive** (cough suppression)
    - Codeine (an opiate derivative) blocks coughing.
- Anti-diarrhea

### SIDE EFFECTS

However, there are several side effects that at times outweigh the use of the drug, including:

- Constipation
- Drowsiness
- Mental closure
- Respiratory depression
- Nausea
- Itching
- Inability to urinate
- Drop in blood pressure
- Constricted pupils, and blurred vision
- Flushed skin

Opiates are a curious family that has legitimate and illegitimate uses. The administration of these drugs ranges from intravenous to oral.

## USES

The uses span from the legal to the illegal. Opiates are used in:

- Medical
- Combat
- Abusers

### MEDICAL

They are often used for pain relief (analgesics), anti-cough medicines (antitussive), and treating diarrhea. The most common clinical use of opiates is to relieve pain.

### COMBAT

During combat, troop medics dose morphine to wounded soldiers. This is a controversial application of the drug, because many soldiers have returned to the states addicted to opiates.

### ABUSE

There is a high risk for addiction for opiates because of the profound sense of euphoria and increased tolerance. Because tolerance happens quickly it is often difficult to determine if an overdose was accidental or suicidal.

Heroin and other opiates are administered in several ways:

- Heavy abusers inject heroin through the veins (**"mainlining"**).
  - Heroin is mixed with lemon juice or other acid to dissolve the substance in water.
  - The acids will erode the veins, and they collapse from the injections after time, and the user finds new veins to inject.
  - The intravenous injection induces euphoria within 30 seconds.
- Injections into the muscle and under the skin.
  - Intramuscular and subcutaneous injections take effect in 3-5 minutes.
- Recreational users typically snort.
  - Snorting is smoking the vapors when heated.
  - When heroin is heated it turns into a thick liquid (like wax), and the user will inhale the smoke through a tube.
  - The user follows the blob of heroin with the tube inhaling as much as possible – called "chasing the dragon."
  - Snorting takes effect in 3-5 minutes.

Heroin is a Schedule I drug in the United States and is not approved for any clinical use. However, it is the most widely abused illegal drug in the world.

## TOLERANCE

To counteract the rapid tolerance and curb some of the side effects sometimes abusers mix drugs.

- Fentanyl is a potentially lethal combination with heroin.
  - Gives the drug a higher potency.
  - Known as "**tango and cash**" or "**goodfellas.**"
- Heroin is used with CNS stimulants to curb drowsiness.
- Crack cocaine smokers will turn to heroin to ease the jitters by smoking a heroin and crack mix (moon rock, parachute rock).
- If 65 milligrams of heroin is taken over a two-week period the user will become physically dependent on heroin.

## WITHDRAWAL SYNDROME

Withdrawal happens quickly:

- 6-12 hours after the last heroin dose symptoms:
  - Runny nose
  - Tears
  - Minor stomach cramps
  - User will feel like they have a cold
  - Sweating
  - Anxiety
- 15-48 hours the symptoms increase
  - Lose appetite
  - Vomit
  - Diarrhea
  - Chills and fever

- 2-4 days the symptoms increase again
  - The user suffers all of the above symptoms.
  - Aching bones and powerful muscle spasms develop.
- 4-5 days the symptoms start to subside
  - The desire to restart heroin is very strong.

Street heroin addicts sometimes use cocaine to withdraw from heroin by gradually decreasing the amounts of heroin while increasing the amounts of cocaine through injection ("**speedballing**") or smoking ("**moon rocks**").

EFFECTS OF OVERDOSE

Death from overdose can take from minutes to hours. Typically the cause is from suppressed respiratory systems, sometimes combined with vomiting by an unconscious user. Overdoses can happen for several reasons including:
- Unknown purity
  - Street heroin purity is unpredictable.
- Unknown dose
- Diminished tolerance
  - Can happen after a period of abstinence.
- Interactions with other depressant drugs
  - Alcohol
  - Benzodiazepines

An overdose can be treated by an opioid antagonist injection. The antagonistic drug (**naloxone** or **naltrexone**) blocks the opioid receptors in the body and will reverse the narcotic effects. The treatment for an overdose will give the person a recurrence of pain they were masking, restore consciousness, normal breathing, and present severe withdrawal effects for someone with strong dependence on the drug.

Heroin is one of the most difficult drugs to stop. It is powerfully addictive and tolerance builds quickly.

### TREATMENT

Trained medical personnel conduct treatment of opiate abuse. Since the body becomes physically dependent on opiates quickly, medical personnel typically need to intervene for a successful withdrawal.

## *TREATMENT OF ABUSE*

Methadone can be taken orally once a day to prevent withdrawal and eliminate the need for a user to search for their next high and use filthy hypodermic needles. There are inherent risks of intravenous narcotics use including:
- Hepatitis
- HIV

Methadone's dose lasts about 24 hours and the dosage is slowly tapered. **Methadone maintenance** shows about the same addiction potential as heroin, however it is recommended for those that have failed many times or who have recently relapsed. **Levo-alpha-acetylmethadol (LAAM)** has also been used to treat heroin abusers, the effects are similar to methadone but this substance has a primary benefit of a longer-lasting effect.

Another approach is benzodiazepines (Valium), which may be given to ease the withdrawal symptoms of opiates. The patient must be monitored carefully on this regiment because there are significant risks with benzodiazepines such as;
- Depression
- Seizures
- Cardiac arrest
- Delirium tremens
- Potential for addiction

The life of a heroin user is not an attractive one. The typically heroin user frequents a "shooting gallery." The shooting gallery is a common place where supplies are stashed. The heroin is prepared for injection by:

- Adding water to the white powder
- Shaking over a small flame (to dissolve the powder)
- Dropping through a wad of cotton
- Loading into the syringe for injection

Due to the debilitating habit of heroin and opiate use many heroin addicts are not functioning in society. They are:

- Low level or unemployed
- Living in unstable conditions
- Socializing with other illicit drug users

## PART X. CANNABINOIDS

This portion of the test will account for approximately eight percent of the questions. Part X will cover:

- History and types
- Effects
- Uses and administration
- Tolerance, withdrawal, and overdose
- Prevention and treatment
- Dependency issues

### HISTORY AND TYPES

Marijuana (ganja, cannabis) is the least seriously addicting drug of abuse and is shrouded in controversy. It is derived from the hemp plant Cannabis Sativa.

### HISTORY

Humans have used marijuana before documentation even exists. In the 20th century usage increased because of:

- Recreation

- Religion

- Spiritual

- Medicinal

Marijuana use declined rapidly in the United States when it became illegal in 1937 with the Marijuana Tax Act of 1937. Marijuana, although illegal, has not been considered a narcotic in the United States since 1971.

Cannabis Sativa has female and male plants; after the male plant releases pollen, the plant usually dies (or the cultivators remove it). The main psychoactive agent in the plant is the **THC** (Delta-9-tetrahydrocannabinol). THC is found mostly in the flower tops and upper leaves of the female plant. However, if the male crops are removed before they are able to pollinate the female crops, then a more potent type of marijuana called **sinsemilla** (without seeds) can be derived from the buds. The highest quality marijuana is found in Jamaica, Columbia, and Mexico. Native United States cannabis contains lower concentrations of THC. Several parts of the plant are used to create different types of marijuana.

- **Herbal** form is made from the mature female flowers and sub-tending leaves.

- **Hashish** is made from the sticky resin from the female plant and contains high amounts of THC.
  - Produced in Lebanon, Afghanistan, and Pakistan
  - **Kief**
    - Moroccan hashish containing only glandular heads.
    - Can be pressed together to make hashish.

- **Ganja** is produced from the dried tops of female plants.
  - Produced in India

- **Ditch weed** is the weakest form of marijuana and it is produced from the parts of the plant with the least amount of THC.
  - Sometimes used to put in drinks, teas, and brownie batter.

EFFECTS

Marijuana has sedative and mild mind-altering effects.

### SHORT-TERM EFFECTS

The high on marijuana is relatively mild (lasting about 2-3 hours from a single joint) and when smoked, reached the brain within 14 seconds. A high has several behavioral, physiological, and subjective effects.

- Behavioral
  - Relaxation
  - Impaired memory
  - Impaired physical coordination
- Physiological
  - A single dose can take 30 days to be completely eliminated.
  - Dry mouth
  - Elevated heartbeat
  - Loss of coordination
  - Slower reaction times
  - High-risk people can have heart attacks from cannabis use
  - Red eyes
    - Due to blood vessel constriction
- Subjective
  - Altered perception of space and time
  - Sense of euphoria
  - Pride selves on knowledge of the drug
    - Read monthly issues of High Times or Hemp News
    - Becomes a lifestyle

However, an acute dose can cause anxiety, panic, and/or paranoia. Extreme reactions are known to occur when the drug is unknowingly laced with another drug.

Marijuana is dangerous when driving or operating heavy machinery because it influences hand-eye coordination and reaction time. Regardless, 60-80% of marijuana users drive while under the influence. Alcohol and marijuana taken together are worse on reaction times than either drug taken alone.

## LONG-TERM EFFECTS

Marijuana has long-term effects as well as short-term ones. Long-term effects include:

- Learning impairment
- Heavy users specifically:
  - Have trouble sustaining and shifting attention
  - Have trouble processing information
  - Suffer from **amotivational syndrome** (lack of motivation and reduced productivity)
  - Apathy
  - Poor short-term memory
  - Difficulty concentrating
- Serious damage to the lungs because the cannabis produces more tar than tobacco and it is full of carcinogens.
- Chromosomal and fertility damage.
  - Lower sperm count
  - Reduced libido
- Cerebral atrophy (shrinking brain)
- Lower white cell capacity (lesser ability to fight disease)

## USES AND ADMINISTRATION

Cannabis Sativa is smoked through the dried and crushed leaves, stems, and seeds produced.

### USES

Cannabis is a diverse and controversial drug. Cannabis is used medically and recreationally, and parts of the plant are used for material.

- Medical Use
    - In the United States the medical use of cannabis is controversial.
        - Pain management (in cultures outside the United States)
        - Treatment for pressure associated with glaucoma, but cannot cure the condition. (Unauthorized medical use in the United States)
        - Nausea treatment (usually associated with chemotherapy treatments)
        - Advanced anorexia treatment
- Recreational use
    - Recreationally cannabis is a popular and relatively mild illicit drug.
- Non-drug use
    - The strong woody fibers in the stem make up hemp. Hemp has long been used for clothing and rope.

### ADMINISTRATION

The primary methods of administration for cannabis use are smoking or oral.

- Smoking
    - Joints
        - Crushed marijuana leaves rolled up in cigarette paper

- o Blunt
  - Crushed marijuana leaves rolled up in cigar paper
- o Bongs (water pipe)
  - Marijuana is placed into a screened bowl over airtight water. A stem is used to inhale the fumes after the marijuana is lit.
- Oral
  - o Sometimes baked in brownies or cake batter for oral consumption.

### Tolerance, withdrawal, and overdose

Marijuana is one of the milder illicit drugs with limited effects of tolerance, withdrawal, and overdose.

#### Tolerance

Tolerance of marijuana builds rapidly. The result of tolerance is a less intense high with repeated administrations.

#### Withdrawal

Withdrawal from marijuana is not recognized by the DSM-IV publication because the medical community does not believe it is a common occurrence. Some reported withdrawal symptoms are (typically rebound symptoms):

- Aggression
- Anger
- Anxiety
- Decreased appetite and weight loss
- Irritability
- Restlessness

#### Overdose

High doses of marijuana can cause unpleasant effects, including:

- Hallucinations
- Delusions
- Paranoia

However, overdose on marijuana is typically not life threatening.

### PREVENTION AND TREATMENT

While the effects of marijuana are relatively mild they can have serious consequences according to the gateway drug theory. The **gateway drug theory** opines that marijuana, tobacco, or alcohol use can lead to more serious drug use. Marijuana use initiates novice users into the drug-using world. Diagnosing marijuana use is usually characterized by a compulsive interest in the drug and significant time spent acquiring the substance.

### PREVENTION

Prevention is most effective with peer groups. Typically marijuana users will associate with other marijuana users. Users typically **"mature out"** of marijuana use by leaving the drug-using groups or behaviors.

### TREATMENT

Treatment for marijuana is usually psychological intervention including:

- Family therapy
- Behavioral therapy
- Community reinforcement

Marijuana abuse appears to be one that is most commonly found in young people ages 18-34. People that abuse marijuana typically thinks and act similarly to those in the same subcultural group **(differential reinforcements)**. Users can exhibit mild physical and psychological dependence:

- Physical
    - For heavy users only and the dependence is mild
- Psychological
    - Deep attachment to the euphoric feelings
    - Craving of the drug when not high

## PART XI. HALLUCINOGENS

This portion of the test will account for approximately four percent of the questions. Part XI will cover:

- History and types
- Effects
- Uses and administration
- Tolerance, withdrawal, and overdose
- Prevention and treatment
- Dependency issues

### HISTORY AND TYPES

**Hallucinogens** pretty much do as the name suggests. They are drugs that produce perceived distortions in reality. The most common types are lysergic acid diethylamide (LSD) (acid), mescaline (from peyote cactus plant), and psilocybin (mushroom, or shroom). **Psychoactive drugs** (psychotropic drugs) can be stimulants, depressants, hallucinogens, opiates, or inhalants. They are identified by their ability to change behavior, feelings, perceptions, and moods.

#### HISTORY

Hallucinogens are ancient drugs that have been used primarily in animistic religious rituals. Prior to the 1930s Native Americans used the mescaline and peyote cactus as hallucinogens without restriction. When peyote was outlawed in the United States an exception was made for the Native American church.

Timothy Leary, a Harvard professor, believed you could reach your inner self through the use of hallucinogens (specifically LSD). He thought that if you had the right setting, dosage, and psychological professionals that behavior could be altered. Most of Leary's research subjects reported that the LSD experiences altered their lives in a very positive way. Leary was fired from Harvard for his use of hallucinogens, and the public attention it garnered. In 1966, Leary founded the League for Spiritual Discovery, a religion claiming LSD as its only sacrament to try to maintain legal status for the use of LSD.

Hallucinogens can be divided into three broad categories:

- Psychedelics
    - Lysergic acid diethylamide ("LSD," "acid," "blotter," "microdot," "white lightning")
        - Main psychedelic
        - Illegal operations in San Francisco are the main source of LSD in the United States.
        - Odorless and tasteless
    - Active ingredients in the Psilocybe mushrooms (**psilocybin, psilocin**)
    - Active ingredients of cacti (Peyote, Sand Pedro, Peruvian Torch cacti) **mescaline**
- **Dissociatives**
    - Blocks signals to conscious mind (typically the senses)
    - Phencyclidine (PCP)
        - Amphetamine like structure
        - Extremely dangerous drug
    - Ketamine
    - Dextromethorphan (DXM)
    - Laughing gas (nitrous oxide)
    - Muscimol (from the amanita muscaria mushroom)
- **Deliriants**
    - Characterized by stupor, confusion, confabulation, and holding conversations with hallucinations.
    - Solanaceae plants (deadly nightshade, mandrake, henbane, sopalia, and datura).
    - Antihistamine diphenhydramine (Benadryl) and Dramamine.
    - Nutmeg in high doses.

Effects vary depending upon the type, dosage, and setting. The drugs can cause **synesthesia**, which is the mixing of senses (e.g., being able to hear a painting, or taste a song).

PSYCHEDELICS

- "Trips" range from short and intense, to days. No two trips are the same.
    - Sometimes flashbacks happen of trips and are pleasant and considered "free trips."
    - Flashbacks can happen as long as five years after a trip (although it isn't common).
- Dosage ranges from very low (LSD) to high (mescaline).
- Relaxation (a feeling of being high on marijuana with enhanced visual perception).
- Euphoria.
- Radiance in colors, with the appearance of objects rippling or breathing. Can become curved, and objects appear strange.
- Distracted and enhanced thought patterns.
- Loss of time sense.
- Can mimic schizophrenia (psychotomimetic).
- Expand or heighten consciousness.

DISSOCIATIVES

- Blocks signals to the conscious mind from other parts of the brain.
- Out of touch with reality.
- High toxicity in many of the dissociatives that can cause death.
- Lucid dreaming with awareness that it is a dream state.
- Uncomfortable side effects:
    - Drying of sweat, saliva, mucus, and urination.

o Dilation of pupils that can last several days causing blurred vision, inability to read, and light sensitivity.

- PCP is the most dangerous (Schedule II drug)

  o Can mimic schizophrenia and catatonia.

  o Can cause euphoria, bizarre perceptions, paranoia, aggression, and can be stored in the cells for many months after ingestion.

DELIRIANTS

- Called true hallucinogens

  o People see things and interact with things that aren't there.

- Side effects include:

  o Pupil dilation

  o Dehydration

PHYSIOLOGICAL EFFECTS

- Hallucinogens are absorbed into all tissues (including the placenta and fetus of a pregnant woman).

- One percent of the dose is received in the brain.

  o Concentrates in the hypothalamus

- Activates sympathetic nervous system

  o Body temperature increases

  o Heart rate rises

  o Blood pressure rises

  o Sweating

  o Pupil dilation

- No physical dependence occurs

ADVERSE PSYCHOLOGICAL EFFECTS

- Psychological dependence can develop

- Nightmarish experiences

- Loss of emotional control

- Paranoid delusions and hallucinations

- Panic attacks

- Tolerance
- Cravings
- Long term problems with memory, speech, and thinking (can last 6-12 months).

Minor hallucinogen:

- **Anticholinergic hallucinogens –**
  - Hallucinogen from the potato family both peripheral and central effects
  - Mucous, saliva, and perspiration levels drop
  - Heart rate decreases
  - Body temperature increases
  - Pupils dilate (difficulty focusing)
  - High doses cause confusion, toxic psychosis. No vivid sensory effect

## Uses and administration

### Uses

There is very little medical approval for hallucinogens. Nitrous Oxide (laughing gas) is sometimes used for dental procedures. Native Americans use hallucinogens sometimes for religious ceremonies. However, the bulk of hallucinogen use is by recreational users.

### Administration

Hallucinogens are administered several ways including:

- Smoking
- Through the skin
- Orally
- Gas inhalation
- Snorting
- Injection

## Tolerance, withdrawal, and overdose

### Tolerance

With the possible exception of PCP, tolerance does not appear to quickly develop from hallucinogens.

### Withdrawal

Since hallucinogens do not seem to be physically addictive there is little documentation of withdrawal symptoms.

### Overdose

Hallucinogen overdose can cause:

- Muscle spasms
- Seizures
- Coma
- Ruptured blood vessels in the brain, heart, or lungs
- Psychosis
- Death

Treatment for an overdose includes:

- Limited contact
- Quiet environment
- Valium

## PREVENTION AND TREATMENT

### PREVENTION

Managing peer groups and instilling a dislike toward drug use is the best prevention.

### TREATMENT

Treatment for hallucinogen use includes:

- Detoxification
- Counseling
- Therapy

### DEPENDENCY ISSUES

Physical dependence for hallucinogens does not occur; however, psychological dependence can develop. People that are more prone to psychological dependency are:

- Mentally ill
  - Depression or bipolar disorders
- Family history of abuse
- Users of other drugs

## PART XII. OTHER DRUGS OF ABUSE

This portion of the test will account for approximately five percent of the questions. Part XII will cover:

- Anabolic steroids
- Over-the-counter substances
- Herbal substances
- Club drugs
- Other prescriptions drugs of interest

### ANABOLIC STEROIDS

Anabolic steroids are abused for muscle production and sports performance. These drugs affect the endocrine (hormonal) system. The endocrine major glands (**pituitary** and **master** gland) regulate the hormones in the body. The **hypothalamus** helps control the activity in the pituitary gland. Steroids are naturally released from the kidney's cortex and medulla to respond to stressful situations. Hormones (testosterone and progesterone) are mostly dormant until puberty. At puberty these hormones become active and help develop and maintain the secondary sex characteristics.

The abuse of steroids results in many unpleasant side effects including:

- Change in liver
- Change in reproductive system
    - Infertility
    - Breast enlargement in males
    - Breast reduction in females
- Skin problems
    - Severe acne
    - Male baldness
- Psychological issues
    - Craving
    - Irritability
    - Outbursts of anger
    - Mania

- o Psychosis
- o Depression
- Changes in cardiovascular system
  - o Increase in blood cholesterol

There are three patterns of steroid abuse:

- Stacking
  - o Using several types of steroids together
- Cycling
  - o Use of different types separately in sequence
- Plateauing
  - o Developing tolerance to the effects of steroids

OVER-THE-COUNTER (OTC) SUBSTANCES

The general view for OTC substances is that they have minimal effects, and are relatively free from side effects. As people become more interested in self-treatment there has been a significant push on the Federal Drug Administration (FDA) to switch some prescription drugs to OTC status. However, OTC drugs are not without their dangers. OTC drugs can cause physical and psychological dependence.

OTC drugs include:

- Decongestants (including antihistamines for relief of allergy symptoms)
    - Antitussive (blocks coughing)
        - Abused because high doses can have PCP like effect.
    - Expectorants (makes coughing more productive)
- Laxatives (relieve constipation)
    - Sometimes abused for weight loss
- Sleep aids
    - Abused to fall asleep or given to underage children to induce sleep.
- Analgesics (pain relief and widest used OTC drug in the United States) and anti-inflammatory
- Stimulants
    - Used to fight fatigue but causes anxiety, restlessness, headaches, rapid heartbeat (tachycardia), and breathing difficulties.
- Cold remedies
- Anti-asthmatics
- Nicotine patches
- Heartburn medication
- Antifungals
- Diet drugs
    - Tolerance quickly develops

The following general rules should be used when taking OTC drugs:

- Know what you are taking
- Know the effects
- Read and heed the warnings
- Don't use more than two weeks
- Be cautious if you are taking prescription medication
- Go to a pharmacist for assistance
- Don't take anything you don't need

There is little to no federal regulation on the herbal substance industry due to a 1994 federal regulation. The government must prove that a substance is harmful before it can be removed from the market. People often mistakenly believe that all herbal supplements are safe because they are natural. Below are some common herbal supplements and their effects on the system.

- Herbal stimulants (ephedrine, ma huang)
  - o Effects include insomnia, heart attacks, strokes, tremors, seizures
- **Milk thistle** (silybum marianum)
  - o Used for liver problems, protect the liver from viruses, toxins, alcohol, and acetaminophen (aspirin).
  - o Some testing has also indicated that milk thistle can inhibit the growth of cancer.
- **Echinacea** (eck-in-A-shuh) looks like a hedgehog (Echinacea is Greek for hedgehog).
  - o Native Americans used echinacea as a general cure-all.
  - o It has been used to treat scarlet fever, syphilis, malaria, and blood poisoning.
  - o Today's use of Echinacea is for reducing the symptoms of flu and cold, and as an immune booster.
- **Ginkgo biloba**
  - o Typically its use is not in the crude, but the extracted state.
  - o It is used to treat circulatory disorders and enhance memory.
  - o Scientific studies suggest ginkgo may be effective in increasing blood flow to the brain of elderly individual.
  - o Ginkgo can also improve blood circulation by dilating the vessels and reducing the adhesive components of the blood platelets.
  - o Ginkgo has flavonoids and terpenoids that are considered antioxidants.
    - ▪ **Antioxidants** neutralize free radicals. **Free radicals** are compounds that

113

alter cell membranes, damage DNA, and can cause death. Free radicals are natural in the body, but can be increased by environmental factors (pollution, smoking, ultraviolet light, and radiation). Free radicals are contributors to heart disease, Alzheimer's disease, and dementia.

- **St. John's wort** (Hypericum perforatum)
  - Used in ancient Greece to treat a range of nervous conditions.
  - It also has antibacterial, antiviral, and anti-inflammatory properties that can help heal wounds and burns.
  - Scientific research suggests St. John's wort can help with depression symptoms as well.

**Designer drugs,** also called "club drugs", produce mild hallucinogenic effects. Teens and young adults in party atmospheres typically abuse these drugs. These drugs include:

- Gamma-hydroxybutyrate (GHB)
    - Date rape drug (when mixed with alcohol the unknowing victim cannot fight off sexual assault)
- Rohypnol (flunitrazepam)
    - Similar to Valium or Xanax
    - Usually taken orally
    - Can be lethal when mixed with alcohol
- Ketamine
    - Usually snorted or injected
- MDMA (Ecstasy)
    - When sold on the street it is often combined with dextromethorphan and caffeine for heightened effect.
    - Side effects such as muscle pain and paranoia
- **Chloral hydrate** is a drug that, slipped into a person's drink, makes someone unconscious.

Prescription drugs are viewed as more potent than OTC drugs and more dangerous. There are several categories of prescription drugs including:

- Analgesics
    - Anti-inflammatory and pain relieving drugs
    - Including Darvon, Percocet, and Demerol
- Antibiotics
    - Used to control infections
    - Penicillin group
- Antidepressants
    - Depression is the most common psychiatric disorder.
    - Monoamine Oxidase (MAO) inhibitors used to treat severe depression.
    - Prozac used to treat mild depression.
- Anti-diabetic drugs
    - Diabetes is a disease caused by elevated blood sugar due to insufficient activity in the pancreas.
        - Type I is a total destruction of insulin producing cells and usually begins in childhood. Type I's are treated with injections of insulin 1-3 times a day.
        - Type II is usually related to obesity and other lifestyle factors where the pancreas is unable to respond properly to keep the blood sugar stable.

## PART XIII. ANTIPSYCHOTIC DRUGS

This portion of the test will account for approximately four percent of the questions. Part XIII will cover:

- History and types
- Effects
- Uses and administration

### HISTORY AND TYPES

Antipsychotics have been available for people with major psychotic medical conditions (schizophrenia) since the mid-1950s. In the 1990s a new brand of antipsychotics called "atypical antipsychotics" were introduced.

- Antipsychotics (Haldol, Thorazine)
    - Original antipsychotics developed for the treatment of severe mental conditions.
- Atypical antipsychotics (Clozaril, Abilify, Risperdal, Zyprexa)
    - Newer antipsychotics developed that appear more effective, but have more severe side effects.

### EFFECTS

The effects of antipsychotics do not produce a high but help alleviate the symptoms of **schizophrenia** (a debilitating mental illness associated with delusions, paranoia, and hallucinations) and other severe psychotic medical conditions.

Side effects with these drugs are also common including:

- Lethargy
- Seizures
- Tremors
- White blood cells hindered against infection

A physician closely monitors dosage for antipsychotics because the dosage varies greatly in individuals. The goal of the medication is to reduce symptoms without producing side effects. Doctors use antipsychotics to treat:

- Schizophrenia
- Mania
- Delusional disorder
- Psychotic depression
- Tourette Syndrome
- Asperger's Syndrome

## Part XIV. Anti-depressants and Mood Stabilizers

This portion of the test will account for approximately four percent of the questions. Part XIV will cover:

- History and types
- Effects
- Uses and administration
- Tolerance, withdrawal, and suicidal behaviors

### History and types

Antidepressants are used for people who have depression. They are sometimes referred to as:

- Selective serotonin reuptake inhibitors
  - Citalopram (Celexa)
  - S-citalopram (Lexapro)
  - Fluoxetine (Prozac)
  - Paroxetine (Paxil, Pexeva)
  - Sertraline (Zoloft)
- Tricyclic antidepressants
  - Amitriptyline (Elavil)
  - Desipramine (Norpramin)
  - Imipramine (Tofranil)
  - Nortriptyline (Aventyl, Pamelor)
- Serotonin and norepinephrine reuptake inhibitors (SNRIs)
  - Venlafaxine (Effexor)
  - Duloxetine (Cymbalta)
- Combined reuptake inhibitors and receptor blockers
  - Trazodone (Desyrel)
  - Nefazodone (Serzone)
  - Maprotiline
  - Mirtazapine (Remeron)
- Monoamine oxidase inhibitors (MAOIs)

o   Isocarboxazid (Marplan)

o   Phenelzine (Nardil)

o   Tranlcypromine (Parnate)

EFFECTS

Antidepressants can take up to several weeks to help with depression symptoms. Some side effects of depression medications are:

- Tiredness

- Insomnia

- Nausea

They work by slowing the removal of certain chemicals (neurotransmitters) from the brain. Therefore, they are more readily available.

Antidepressants can have effects on other medicines. Therefore, talking to a pharmacist or doctor about current medical regimes is important before taking antidepressants.


USES AND ADMINISTRATION

**Depression** is an overwhelming feeling of worthlessness, despair, and sadness that exaggerates reality. It is one of the most common psychological disorders. There are two types of depression; it is important to understand the types because each has a different treatment.

- In **primary depression** the individual experiences onset for no apparent reason.
    o   Primary depression is usually attributed to brain chemistry.
    o   The most successful treatment for primary depression is antidepressants.
    o   Doctors prescribe antidepressants usually for 4 to 6 months (in some cases longer).
- **Secondary depression**, also known as **reactive depression**; onset can be clearly identified to a traumatic event (e.g., death, divorce).
    o   The most successful treatment for secondary depression is counseling and other therapies.

LIST OF APPENDICES

| Appendix | Description |
|---|---|
| Appendix A | Approximate Percentages of the Examination |
| Appendix B | Potency of Cannabis Sativa |
| Appendix C | Drug Prevention |
| Appendix D | Stages of Change Model |

| Percentage | Curriculum Content |
| --- | --- |
| 11% | **Overview of Substance Abuse and Dependence Abuse**<br>• Terminology<br>• Theories of Abuse and Dependence<br>• Models of Abuse and Dependence<br>• Demographics<br>• Costs to Society and Associations with Social Problems<br>• Screening and Diagnosis |
| 6% | **Classification of Drugs** |
| 11% | **Pharmacological and Neurophysiological Principles**<br>• Nervous System<br>• Actions of Drugs<br>• Drug Interactions |
| 12% | **Alcohol**<br>• History and Types<br>• Determinants of Blood Alcohol Level<br>• Effects<br>• Uses and Administration<br>• Tolerance, Withdrawal, and Overdose<br>• Dependency Issues<br>• Prevention and Treatment |
| 6% | **Anti-anxiety and Sedative Hypnotics**<br>• History and Types<br>• Effects<br>• Uses and Administration<br>• Tolerance, Withdrawal, and |

| Percentage | Curriculum Content |
|---|---|
| | Overdose<br>• Dependency Issues<br>• Prevention and Treatment |
| 4% | **Inhaled Substances**<br>• History and Types<br>• Effects<br>• Uses and Administration<br>• Tolerance, Withdrawal, and Overdose<br>• Dependency Issues<br>• Prevention and Treatment |
| 7% | **Tobacco and Nicotine**<br>• History and Types<br>• Effects<br>• Uses and Administration<br>• Tolerance, Withdrawal, and Overdose<br>• Dependency Issues<br>• Prevention and Treatment |
| 9% | **Psychomotor Stimulants**<br>• History and Types<br>• Effects<br>• Uses and Administration<br>• Tolerance, Withdrawal, and Overdose<br>• Dependency Issues<br>• Prevention and Treatment |
| 9% | **Opioids**<br>• History and Types<br>• Effects<br>• Uses and Administration<br>• Tolerance, Withdrawal, and Overdose<br>• Dependency Issues |

| Percentage | Curriculum Content |
|---|---|
| | • Prevention and Treatment |
| 8% | **Cannabinoids**<br>• History and Types<br>• Effects<br>• Uses and Administration<br>• Tolerance, Withdrawal, and Overdose<br>• Dependency Issues<br>• Prevention and Treatment |
| 4% | **Hallucinogens**<br>• History and Types<br>• Effects<br>• Uses and Administration<br>• Tolerance, Withdrawal, and Overdose<br>• Dependency Issues<br>• Prevention and Treatment |
| 5% | **Other Drugs of Abuse**<br>• Anabolic Steroids<br>• Over-the-Counter (OTC) Substances<br>• Herbal Substances<br>• Club Drugs<br>• Other Prescription Drugs of Interest |
| 4% | **Antipsychotic Drugs**<br>• History and Types<br>• Effects<br>• Uses and Administration |

| Percentage | Curriculum Content |
|---|---|
| 4% | **Antidepressants and Mood Stabilizers**<br>• History and Types<br>• Effects<br>• Uses and Administration<br>• Tolerance Withdrawal and Suicidal Behaviors |

APPENDIX B: POTENCY OF CANNABIS SATIVA

| Potency of THC in Cannabis (Descending order) |
|---|
| Trichomes |
| Female flowers |
| New shoots |
| Leaves from flowers |
| Leaves in ascending order of size |
| Stems of leaves (peioles) in ascending order of size |
| Stems in ascending order of size |
| Roots and seeds |

| Level | Characteristics |
|---|---|
| Primary | • Very broad range of activity aimed at reducing risk of drug use from even starting.<br>• Assumes people targeted are nonusers and wish to keep them that way. |
| Secondary | • Targets at-risk groups, experimenters, and early abusers.<br>• Attempt to reverse progression of abuse. |
| Tertiary | • Intervention at an advanced state of drug abuse.<br>• Drug abuse treatment. |

| Level | Characteristics |
|---|---|
| Precontemplation | • Not acknowledging a problem.<br>• Not interested in help.<br>• Defend current habits. |
| Contemplation | • Acknowledgement of problem, but unsure if willing to make change.<br>• Thinking about giving up the habit, but unsure if willing to do so. |
| Preparation/Determination | • Getting ready to change.<br>• Small steps toward quitting. |
| Action/Willpower | • People believe they have the ability to change.<br>• Use different techniques to change it. |
| Maintenance | • Being able to abstain from the substance. |
| Relapse | • Return to old behaviors.<br>• Typically, during quitting there is at least one relapse. |
| Transcendence | • Able to abstain and maintain maintenance.<br>• Able to live and process emotions without the use of substances. |

# GLOSSARY

Because this is a study guide, some of these words are found throughout the text, however there are some new ones, be sure you understand the meanings to all of these words because they will help you exponentially during the multiple choice test… Remember what you can, make flashcards for the rest, and quiz yourself a lot, you won't regret it!

## A

**Absorption -** how the drug moves from administration to the system it is supposed to effect

**Abstinence-** discontinuance and avoidance of a drug

**Activation -** how a drug is used to produce an effect

**Acute** – immediate reaction to a drug

**Addictive Personality-** an addictive personality is a trait that presents itself in response to habit-forming drugs/alcohol or compulsive behavior.

**Additive drug effect -** drugs combine in the system, but they do not exaggerate one another

**Administration -** how a drug is introduced into the body

**Adulterated** – mixing drugs with other ingredients such as powdered sugar, talc, arsenic, methamphetamine, or lidocaine

**Adverse Reaction-** unintended (bad) reaction to a drug

**AIDS** – Acquired Immunodeficiency Syndrome contracted by blood (risk of intravenous drug use)

**Alcoholics Anonymous (AA)** – started in 1935 to help people recover from alcoholism in a 12-step program that relies on faith

**Alcoholic cardiomyopathy**- congestive heart failure due to the replacement of heart muscle with fat and fiber

**Alcohol dehydrogenase** - enzyme that metabolizes ethanol

**Alcoholic hepatitis** - the second stage of alcohol-induced liver disease in which chronic inflammation occurs

**Alcohol poisoning** - (acute alcohol intoxication) potentially fatal condition that is caused by the rapid increase in the BAC level due to consumption of alcoholic beverages

**Alternatives approach** – belief that explores positive alternatives to drug abuse to try to fill the same need (pleasure)

**Amphetamine** - behavioral stimulant

**Amotiviational syndrome** – idea that heavy marijuana use causes lack of ambition

**Analgesics** - pain relief drug

**Analog** – drugs with similar chemical structures

**Anemia** – low iron in blood

**Anhedonia** – lock of emotional response (no joy or pleasure)

**Anorexiants** – drugs that suppress the appetite

**Antabuse** - drug that blocks the metabolism of alcohol and any alcohol will cause very unpleasant symptoms (headache, flushing, nausea)

**Antagonistic drug effect** - when one drug cancels the effect of another

**Antecedent** – variable before drug use

**Anticholinergic hallucinogens** – hallucinogen from the potato family

**Antitussive** - cough suppression drug

**Array** – use of other drugs with steroids to avoid side effects

**Aspiration** - vomiting while unconscious

**Athetosis** –jerkiness of limbs, side effect of some drugs

**Attitude change model** – assumes people use drugs because of low self-esteem

**Aversive conditioning** – little used form of behavioral therapy that pairs an unpleasant side effect with an undesired behavior

## B

**Barbiturates -** potent CNS depressants (sedative hypnotics), usually not preferred because of their narrow margin of safety

**Behavioral tolerance** -compensation for motor impairments through behavioral pattern modification by alcoholics

**Behavioral stereotypy** – single meaningless activity repeated

**Behaviorism-** branch of psychology that bases its observations and conclusions on definable and measurable behavior

**Biological explanation of abuse** - focuses heavily on the reward sensors found in the CNS (they are more sensitive in a users CNS to their drug of choice)

**Biotransformation** - process of changing chemical properties of a drug (typically the liver)

**Blood Alcohol Level or Concentration (BAC)** - concentration of alcohol in the blood

**Bootlegging** - selling homemade illegal alcohol through underground channels

**Buergers's disease** - (thromboangiitis) is a recurring inflammation and thrombosis (clotting) in arteries and veins in hands and feet, caused by the reduction of blood to the body's extremities. Associated with tobacco products.

## C

**Cannabis sativa (Marijuana, Hashish)** – the dried leaves, flowers, stems, and seeds of the Cannabis Sativa Plant

**Carboxyhemoglobin** - carbon monoxide that smoking generates combines with red blood cells rendering the red blood cells inert

**Carcinogen** – substance or agent that can cause cancer

**Catatonia** – state of rigidity, stupor, or excitement

**Causal factors-** conditions that influence the outcome of a chemical dependency problem in an individual

**Central Nervous System (CNS)-** The brain and spinal cord

**Chasing the dragon** – when crack cocaine users will turn to heroin to ease the jitters by smoking a heroin and crack mix (moon rock, parachute rock)

**Chemical dependence** - synonymous with Substance Abuse

**Chloral hydrate-** drug that makes someone unconscious (can be slipped into a drink)

**Chloroform** – drug initially used for anesthetic, but has largely been replaced

**Chronic** – long term reaction to a drug

**COLD (Chronic Obstructive lung Disease)** - Inflammation or infection of the small airways that go into the lungs

**Chippers** – see "floaters"

**Cirrhosis** - scarring of the liver and formation of fibrous tissues; results from alcohol abuse

**Classical conditioning-** learning an association between two stimuli (discovered by Pavlov)

**Closed meetings** – meeting where alcoholics with a serious desire to quit are the only ones that can come

**Club drug** – drugs used at raves, parties, and dance clubs to enhance experience (MDMA (Ecstasy), GHB, Rohypnol, katmine, methamphetamine, and LSD)

**Cocaine "bugs"** – symptom of cocaine withdrawal that feels like insects crawling all over the body.

**Cocathylene** – chemical formed with ethanol and cocaine

**Co-Dependence** - a person takes responsibility for actions
of others and helps avoid facing problems directly
in order to preserve stability in a family relationship
(enabler)

**Codeine**- sedative and analgesic agent found in opium

**Cognitive therapy** - form of psychotherapy based on the
belief that psychological problems are the products
of faulty perspectives

**Conditioning** - change in behavior due to association
between events.

**Congestion rebound**- withdrawal from use of
decongestant, resulting in severe congestion

**Congestive heart failure** – heart is unable to pump
sufficient blood to the body

**Crack** - the form of cocaine that is processed into rock
crystals and heated

**Cross-dependence** - dependence on a drug can be relieved
by other similar drugs

**Cross- tolerance** – tolerance in one drug can cause
increased tolerance of another drug that is closely
related.

**Cycling** – use of different steroids in sequence

**Crystal meth** (ice)- the most dangerous methamphetamine

**Cumulative effect**- buildup of a drug in the body after
multiple doses taken at short intervals

### D

**DARE** – Drug Abuse Resistance Education geared toward
children (primary prevention)

**DEA-** Drug Enforcement Administration/division of the U.S. Department of Justice

**Deliriants-** characterized by stupor, confusion, confabulation, and holding conversations with hallucinations

**Delirium tremens-** the most severe, can be life-threatening, form of alcohol withdrawal, involving hallucinations, delirium, and fever

**Denial** - refusal to admit to one's self the truth or reality

**Depression** - state of sadness marked by inactivity and inability to concentrate

**Depressant** - any of several drugs that sedate by acting on the central nervous system

**Designer drugs** – drugs designed to mimic the effects of illicit drugs and controlled substances.

**Detoxification** - removal of a drug or alcohol from the body

**Dextromethorphan** – OTC cough suppressant ingredient

**Differential association** – process where individuals are socialized into perceptions and values of a group

**Differential reinforcement** - ratio between reinforcers, both favorable and unfavorable, for sustaining drug use behavior

**Disease model** – belief that people abuse alcohol because alcoholism is a disease

**Dispositional tolerance** – increased use of drug causes an increase in the rate of metabolism for that drug. Therefore, more of the drug is necessary to maintain the drug in the body.

**Dissociatives** - blocks signals to conscious mind (typically the senses)

**Distillation** - heating fermented mixtures of cereal grains or fruits in a still to evaporate and be trapped as purified alcohol

**Distribution** -how the drug moves to various areas in the body

**Ditch weed** - weakest form of marijuana and it is produced from the parts of the plant with the least amount of THC

**Doping** – using performance enhancing drugs to enhance athletic ability

**Dose response** - correlation between the amount of a drug given and its effects

**Downers** – see depressants

**Drug** – any substance that modifies the bodily functions

**Drug abuse** – the intentional misuse of any drug

**Drug addiction** – a physiological and psychological need for drug abuse

**Drug misuse**- the unintentional misuse of prescribed or over the counter drugs (i.e. taking more than prescribed, stopping a medicine before prescribed, or sharing medicines)

**Drug tolerance**- decreased responsiveness to a drug

**Dual-diagnosis**- describes condition of mental patients who are also addicted to a mind-altering drug

**DUI** - Driving under the influence of alcohol or an illicit substance - any substance, licit or illicit, if it impairs the driving function

**DWI**- Driving While Intoxicated

**Dysphoric**- unpleasant effects opposite of euphoric

**E**

**Echinacea** – herbal general cure all

**ED50** – effective dose for half animals tested

**Elimination** - how a drug metabolizes out of the body

**Enabling** - loved ones refusal to admit drinking is a problem

**Endorphins-** the body's natural euphoric hormones

**Enkephalins** – morphine-like neurotransmitters

**Entactogens** – drugs that enhance the sense of touch

**Enzyme** – molecule that assists synthesis of another molecule

**Ergogenic** – drugs that enhance athleticism

**Ergotism** – toxicns in the ergot fungus Claviceps Purpurea

**Ethanol** – drinkable alcohol

**Ethylene glycol** – anti-freeze

**F**

**Fermentation**- produces ethanol or ethyl alcohol when yeast converts sugars

**Fetal Alcohol Syndrome (FAS)** – physical characteristic birth defects (small birth weight, small head, small eyes, thin upper lip), cardiac abnormalities, and developmental retardation seen in some babies of alcoholic mothers

**Fetal Drug Syndrome (FDS)-** A pattern of developmental birth defects characterized by low birth weight, growth retardation, premature delivery, or spontaneous abortion, and withdrawal symptoms

**Flashbacks** – recurrence of earlier drug induced sensory experiences (without the use of the drug) sometimes referred to as a free high

**Floaters**– light to moderate consumption of drugs (vacillating between chronic and experimental use) aka chippers

**Freebase** -use of powder cocaine chemically altered and smoked through a pipe

## G

**Gamma hyrdoxybutyrate (GHB)** – recreational depressant drug

**Ganja** – marijuana produced from the dried tops of female plants

**Gaseous phase** – the actual smoke (carbon monoxide) from a cigarette

**Gastritis** – acute gastric distress

**Gateway drugs** – substances that typically lead to more severe drugs and heavier usage: the three gateway drugs are alcohol, tobacco, and marijuana

**Genogram** -family therapy technique that records information about behavior and relationships on a type of family tree to clarify patterns of dysfunction

**Ginkgo Biloba** – herbal substance used to treat circulatory disorders and enhance memory

**Glial cell** – specialized cell in nervous system

# H

**Habituation** - repeated patterns until they are well established

**Half-life** - time required for the body to eliminate and/or metabolize half of a drug dose

**Hallucination** - perception of objects or experience of sensations with no real external cause

**Hallucinogen-** chemical substance, which distorts perceptions to induce delusions or hallucinations

**Hashish** - marijuana made from the sticky resin from the female plant and contains high amounts of THC

**Hepatotoxic effect-** alcoholic liver cells increase the production of fat, resulting in an enlarged liver

**HIV-** the human immunodeficiency virus, the causative agent of Acquired Immunodeficiency Syndrome (AIDS)

**Hogsheads** – tobacco packed in wooden barrels

**Homeostasis** – body's strive for stability

**Hypnotics** - CNS depressants used to induce drowsiness and encourage sleep

**Hypoxia** - lack of oxygen

# I

**ICE** – smokable form of methamphetamine

**Illicit drugs** – illegal substances that affect bodily functions (cocaine, marijuana, and others)

**Inhalant** – drug administered through the lungs

**Inoculation** - abuse prevention that protects drug users by teaching them responsibility

**Interdiction** - cutting off or destroying supplies of illicit drugs

**Intoxication-** being under the influence of drugs

**Involuntary smoking-** inhalation of the cigarette smoke of others

## J

**Jimsonweed** – hallucinogenic plant

## K

**Keratolytics** – caustic agents that cause the keratin skin layer to peel

## L

**Labeling theory-** stresses that other people's impression of us has a direct impact on our self-image

**LD50** – lethal dose in half animals tested

**Leukoplakia** -development of white leathery patches on gums, tongue, and inside cheeks caused by tobacco use

**Levo-alpha-acetylmethadol (LAAM)-** used to treat heroin abusers, the effects are similar to methadone but this substance has a primary benefit of a longer-lasting effect

**Lipid solubility** – ability of a chemical to dissolve in fat

# M

**Main effects** – a drugs intended response

**Mainstream smoke** – smoke that comes from the mouthpiece of cigarette, cigar, or pipe

**Margin of safety** -range in dose between the amount of drug necessary to cause a therapeutic effect and that needed to create a toxic effect

**Master status -** overriding position in the eyes of others either positive (doctor, lawyer, police officer), or negative (mental patient, alcoholic, "druggie")

**Mead** - fermented honey often made into an alcoholic beverage; probably the first alcoholic beverage

**Medical Model** - theory of drug abuse or addiction in which the addiction is seen as a medical, rather than as a social problem

**Medicines** – drugs used to treat or prevent an illness prescribed by a medical doctor

**Meninges** - triple-tiered protective coat that layers the CNS

**Methadone**- A synthetically produced, long-acting opiate used to treat heroin addiction

**Methamphetamine -** related to amphetamine, however it is longer lasting and more toxic

**Methyl alcohol** – wood alcohol

**Milk Thistle (silybum marianum)** – herbal substance used for liver problems, protect the liver from viruses, toxins, alcohol and acetaminophen (aspirin)

**Minnesota Model** – treatment of substance abuse involving a month long stay in an inpatient environment with long and short term goals

**Moral model**- belief that people abuse alcohol by choice

**Morphine** - major sedative and analgesic drug found in opium

**Mothers Against Drunk Driving (MADD)** - group focused on alcohol reduction, which was founded by Candy Lightner after her daughter was killed in 1980

**Muscle dysmorphia** – behavioral syndrome in men to have a distorted image of themselves (small, weak, fat, and flabby)

**Mydriasis** – pupil dilation

**N**

**Naloxone** – drug used to treat opiate overdoses

**Narcotic**- drug with ability to produce a state of sleep or drowsiness and to relieve pain with the potential of dependence

**Nerve impulse** - communication that is carried by the neurons is done through an electric-like transmission

**Neuroleptic** – antipsychotic drug

**Neuron** – specialized cell in nervous system

**Neurotransmitter**- natural chemical released by one neuron to influence or communicate with another

**Nicotine**- main active ingredient of tobacco, toxic and causes irritation of lung tissues, constriction of blood vessels, increased blood pressure and heart rate, and central nervous system stimulation

**Nitrous oxide** – laughing gas

# O

**Operant conditioning** - responses become more frequent if followed by satisfying consequences but less frequent if followed by aversive consequences

**Opiate**- substance related in action to morphine and binds to the same, or some of the same, receptors

**Over-the-Counter Drugs-** drugs legally sold without a prescription

# P

**Paraphernalia** – equipment used to administer drugs

**Particulate phase** - particles of the cigarette; nicotine, water, and the chemical compounds (tar)

**Passive smoking** – nonsmoker's inhalation of sidestream smoke

**Pharmacology**- branch of science that deals with the study of drugs and their action on living systems

**Phenothiazines** - drugs that cause psychosis

**Phocomelia** – birth defect of the arms and/or legs

**Physical dependence** – drug dependence based on bodies adaptation to the drug

**Placebo effects** - suggestion and psychological factors independent of the pharmacological activity of a drug

**Plateau effect** – maximum effects (regardless of dose)

**Potency** – strength of drug

**Potentiated drug effect** - when one drug actually intensifies the effect of another

**Potentiation** – see synergism

**Precursor drugs** – chemicals needed to produce a drug

**Prescription drugs-** controlled drug available only by the order of a licensed physician

**Prevention -** Primary, secondary and tertiary-

- **Primary prevention** - active assertive process of creating conditions and or personal attributes that promote the well being of people
- **Secondary prevention -** early detection and intervention to keep beginning problems from becoming more severe
- **Tertiary prevention** - rehabilitate those affected with severe disorders and return them to the community

**Primary deviance** -someone is engaging in a small deviant behavior but does not identify with it. For example, someone experimenting with drugs does not identify himself or herself as a "user".

**Primary prevention** – prevention of any drug use

**Problem drinking** - person doesn't need drinks to support body functions (they aren't psychologically or physically addicted) but when they do drink they cause problems for themselves or others

**Prognosis** - recovery as anticipated from the usual course of a disease

**Prohibition** - laws prohibiting all sales of alcoholic beverages in the United States from 1920 to 1933

**Proof** – measure of alcohol based on twice the alcohol percentage. Example: 100 proof whiskey is 50% alcohol.

**Protease inhibitors** – class of drugs to treat HIV

**Pseudointoxicated** – acting drunk before alcohol has taken effect

**Psilocybin -** the active chemical in Psilocybe mushrooms

**Psychedelic**- mind-altering group of drugs producing a mental state of great calm and euphoria

**Psychoactive drug**- chemical that alters mood or behavior as a result of alterations in the functioning of the brain

**Psychodrama** - a family therapy system developed by Jacques Moreno where issues are enacted in a focused setting using dramatic techniques

**Psychological explanation of drug abuse** - focuses heavily abusers inability to cope with reality and desire to escape

**Psychotherapy**- treatment of emotional or behavioral problems by psychological means, often in one-to-one interviews or small groups

**Pyschotogenic** – substances that initiate psychotic behavior

**Psychotomimetic**- substance that cause psychosis symptoms

**Psychotropic drug**- substance that acts on psychic mood behavior or experience

**Psychological dependence**- compulsion and craving to use a drug for its effects

**Psychopharmacology**- study of the effects of drugs on mood, sensation, consciousness, or other psychological or behavioral functions

**Psychiatrist**- person with a degree in medicine (MD) with additional training in the study of mental disorders

**Pulmonary emphysema** - non-curable disease that destroys the aleveoli (sacs where the air is transferred into the blood) typically caused by smoking

**Pyramiding** – moving from a low dose to a higher dose and reducing at the end of a cycle

## Q

**Quid** - a piece of chewing tobacco

## R

**Rebound effect** -form of withdrawal opposite effects that occur when a drug has been eliminated from the body

**Receptor**- special protein on the membrane or in the cytoplasm of a cell with which a drug, a neurotransmitter, or a hormone interacts

**Recidivism**-return or relapse to a type of behavior, such as drug taking

**Rehabilitate**- to restore to effectiveness or normal life by training especially after imprisonment, drug addiction, or illness

146

**Relapse-** a recurrence of symptoms of the disease after a period of sobriety

**Reverse tolerance-** enhanced response given on same dose (opposite of tolerance)

**Runs** – patterns of high dose and frequent use of amphetamines, can last as long as 15 days

## S

**Saint John's Wort (Hypericum perforatum)** – herbal substance used in ancient Greece to treat a range of nervous conditions

**Schizophrenia -** a debilitating mental illness associated with delusions, paranoia, and hallucinations

**Secondary deviance-** someone begins to identify him or herself with the deviant behavior. For example, someone may start to perceive themselves as drug users and will more likely become an abuser.

**Secondary prevention** – preventing drug use from casual to drug dependence

**Self-help group-** group of individuals with similar problems that meets for the purpose of providing support and information to each other and for mutual problem solving

**Serotonin** – body chemical that's main function is sleep.

**Side effects** - secondary effects, usually undesirable, of a drug or therapy or behavior

**Side stream smoke** - smoke arising from the ash of the cigarette or cigar

**Sinsemilla** – literally "without seeds" marijuana that is made from the buds and flowering tops of the female plants (one of the most potent types)

**Social influence model** – socially abstaining from drugs and making drugs not-OK decreases risk of drug use. (i.e. Just Say No campaign and the new rules and regulations for smoking have both effectively diminished drug use and smoking in the American public).

**Sociobiological changes** – believe that genes have a direct influence on social psychological behavior

**Speed freak** – see "Tweaker"

**Speedballs** – use of heroin and cocaine together

**Spinal cavity** – holds and protects the spinal cord

**Stages of change** - a model for decision-making consisting of precontemplation, contemplation, preparation, action, and maintenance

**Steroids**- is any of a group of solid, cyclic unsaturated alcohols, such as cholesterol, found in plant and animal tissue

**Stimulant**- drugs that act on the central nervous system to produce excitation, alertness and wakefulness

**Straight**- not using drugs

**Students Against Drunk Driving (SADD)**- group that focuses on high school students that enforces a contractual agreement between parent and child

**Switching policy** - an FDA policy changing of suitable prescription drugs to over-the-counter status

**Synaptic cleft** - small gap between neurons

**Synapse** - junction between the neurons

**Synergism**– (aka potentiation) ability of one drug to enhance the effect of another (sum of both is greater than if both were taken separately

**Synesthesia**- mixing of senses (i.e. being able to hear a painting, or taste a song) common with hallucinogens

## T

**Teetotaler-** someone does not drink alcohol for any reason.

**Temperance** – idea that people can consume alcohol in moderation and abstain from hard liquor

**Teratogenic** – drugs that cause physical harm to fetus

**Tertiary drug prevention** – intervention at an advanced state of drug use

**Theobromine** – a xanthine found in chocolate

**Theophylline** – a xanthine found in tea

**Therapeutic community** – drug free residential settings to teach increased responsibility

**Threshold dose** – minimum amount of drug to cause an effect

**Time course** - timing of the onset, duration, and termination of a drug's effect

**Tolerance** – increased dosage needed in order to achieve the same effect

**Toxicity**- the margin between the dosage that produces beneficial effects and the dosage that produces poisonous effects varies with the drug and the person receiving it

**Tranquilizers**- drugs meant to relax or treat psychotic disorders

**Tweaker** - someone who has patterns of high dose and use of amphetamines

## U

**Uppers**- stimulants or amphetamines

**Uptake** – selected molecules taken into cells

## V

**Values -** convictions, or beliefs about the manner in which people should behave and the principles that should govern behavior

**Values clarification -** teaching students to recognize and express their own feelings and beliefs

**Volatile** – evaporated at low temperatures

## W

**Wernicke-Korsakoff syndrome**- brain disorder involving lack of thiamine usually associated with alcohol.

**Withdrawal** - group of reactions or behavior that follows abrupt cessation of the use of a drug upon which the body has become dependent (can be fatal)

## X

**Xanthines** – family of caffeine drugs

If you can answer about half of the questions correctly you should be in good shape. To be safe, strive for a 75% on this examination.

1.  When _____ were outlawed the Native American church was an exception?
    a.  Hallucinogens
    b.  Cannabis Sativa
    c.  Heroin
    d.  Cocaine
    e.  Alcohol

2.  Identifying someone as a doctor, lawyer, or drug addict is an example of his or her:
    a.  Profession
    b.  Societal worth
    c.  Job title
    d.  Master status
    e.  Ability to integrate with upper levels of society

3.  Which of the following is NOT an effect of hallucinogens?
    a.  Loss of emotional control
    b.  Panic attacks
    c.  Paranoid delusions
    d.  Nightmarish experience
    e.  Total relaxation

4.  Withdrawal from stimulants happens in the following three distinct stages:
    a.  Crash, Withdrawal, Extinction
    b.  Withdrawal, Cravings, Extinction
    c.  Crash, Cravings, Withdrawal
    d.  Cravings, Extinction, Relapse
    e.  Withdrawal, Crash, Cravings

5. Which of the following is NOT a way that drug users experience consumption of a drug?
    a. Cultural
    b. Social
    c. Psychological
    d. Contextual
    e. Pharmacological

6. Which of the following typically has the least alcohol content?
    a. United States beer
    b. Wine cooler
    c. Dessert wine
    d. Liquor
    e. Red wine

7. Due to the _____ federal regulation there is little the government can do to intervene upon the sales of herbal substances.
    a. 2000
    b. 1999
    c. 1997
    d. 2002
    e. 1994

8. Which of the following is NOT a sign of fetal alcohol syndrome?
    a. Mental retardation
    b. Facial deformities
    c. Flat face with an upward slant to the eye
    d. Widely set eyes
    e. Joint problems

9. A heroin overdose is treated with:
    a. Methadone
    b. Naloxone
    c. Benzodiazipines
    d. Barbiturates
    e. Antabuse

10. Which of the following is NOT a side effect of anti-psychotics?
    a. Lethargy
    b. Tremors
    c. Seizures
    d. White blood cells hindered against infection
    e. Dilated pupils

11. Which of the following is NOT a club drug?
    a. Gamma hydroxybutyrate (GHB)
    b. Rohypnol (flunitrazepam)
    c. MDMA (ecstasy)
    d. Ketamine
    e. They are all club drugs

12. What herbal remedy is sometimes used to treat depression?
    a. St. John's wort
    b. Ginkgo biloba
    c. Echinacea
    d. Milk thistle
    e. Ma huang

13. How did prohibition affect the American public?
    a. There was an outright disrespect for the law and criminal activity soared.
    b. People turned to religion to justify temperance.
    c. The United State recognized their problem and began to abstain from alcohol and form many help groups (such as AA).
    d. Speakeasies were immediately closed to comply with the law.
    e. Bootlegging was uncommon and the American society remained fairly sober.

14. If someone taking Antabuse has alcohol, what is the likely effect?
    a. Nausea
    b. Nightmares
    c. Tremors
    d. Seizure
    e. Coma

15. What kind of effect is defined as the buildup of a drug in the body after multiple doses taken at short intervals?
    a. Potentiated effect
    b. Cumulative effect
    c. Negated effect
    d. Additional effect
    e. Exponential effect

16. What is homeostasis?
    a. The bodies desire for stability
    b. A plateau in a drug cycle
    c. Two drugs related that create a potentiated effect
    d. Drugs that are related to one another
    e. None of the above

17. Which of the following is crushed marijuana leaves rolled up in cigar paper?
    a. Joint
    b. Blunt
    c. Bong
    d. Cigarette
    e. None of the above

Use the following for questions 18-22
    I.      Echinacea
    II.     St John's Wort
    III.    Ginko Biloba
    IV.     Milk Thistle
    V.      Ma Huang

18. An herbal stimulant:
    a. I
    b. II
    c. III
    d. IV
    e. V

19. Historically used as a general cure-all:
    a. I
    b. II
    c. III
    d. IV
    e. V

20. Herbal substance used to heal cuts and burns:
    a. I
    b. II
    c. III
    d. IV
    e. V

21. Herbal substance used to improve memory:
    a. I
    b. II
    c. III
    d. IV
    e. V

22. Used to treat depression:
    a. I
    b. II
    c. III
    d. IV
    e. V

23. What are the branchlike structures that pick up neuron communications?
    a. Synapse
    b. Dendrites
    c. Axon
    d. Neurotransmitters
    e. Cerebral cortex

24. Which of the following is NOT a factor in Blood Alcohol Concentration (BAC)?
    a. Size of person
    b. Gender
    c. Amount of food in digestive system
    d. Environment of drinking
    e. How closely in time drinks are consumed

25. Which type of alcohol is consumable?
    a. Methanol
    b. Ethanol
    c. Isopropanol
    d. Isobutyl
    e. Phenylethyl

Use the following for questions 26-30
    I.      Schedule I
    II.     Schedule II
    III.    Schedule III
    IV.    Schedule IV
    V.     Schedule V

26. Barbiturates are in this schedule of drugs?
    a. I
    b. II
    c. III
    d. IV
    e. V

27. The DEA monitors the prescription issued in this schedule of drugs:
    a. I
    b. II
    c. III
    d. IV
    e. V

28. There are no accepted medical uses for this schedule of drug:
    a. I
    b. II
    c. III
    d. IV
    e. V

29. Sleeping pills (chloral hydrate) are in this drug category:
    a. I
    b. II
    c. III
    d. IV
    e. V

30. Cough suppressants are in this drug category:
    a. I
    b. II
    c. III
    d. IV
    e. V

31. Wernicke-Korsakoff syndrome is a brain disorder involving lack of _____.
    a. Neurotransmitters
    b. Calcium
    c. Thiamine
    d. Zinc
    e. Vitamin C

32. What is the most widely abused illicit drug:
    a. Coffee
    b. Tobacco
    c. Marijuana
    d. Organic solvents
    e. Hallucinogens

33. Who of the following is LEAST likely to abuse inhalants?
    a. Younger kids
    b. Members of socioeconomically impoverished areas
    c. People in prison
    d. People in institutions
    e. All of the above people are in the high-risk group of using inhalants.

34. Which of the following is the effect that explains the phenomenon where one drug intensifies the effect of another?
    a. Exponential
    b. Antagonistic
    c. Additive
    d. Potentiated
    e. Double-effect

35. Which of the following groups is focused on a contractual agreement between parent and child?
    a. AA
    b. MADD
    c. SADD
    d. DARE
    e. None of the above

36. Benzodiazepines are examples of which kind of drugs?
    a. Cannabis Sativa
    b. Hallucinogens
    c. Opiates
    d. Inhalants
    e. Anti-anxiety

37. Which of the following can be found in the CNS?

      I.      Spinal cavity
      II.     Meninges
      III.    Cerebral Cortex
      IV.    Reticular activating system
      V.     Brain

    a. I and IV
    b. I only
    c. III and IV
    d. II, III, and IV
    e. All of the above

38. Which of the following is NOT a method to increase likelihood of quitting smoking?
    a. Nibble fruits and vegetables
    b. Sleep an additional hour a day
    c. Use mouthwash after meals
    d. Chew gum
    e. Discard smoking paraphernalia

39. Anticholinergic hallucinogens are found in what plant family?
    a. Poppy
    b. Squash
    c. Potato
    d. Cannabis
    e. Coca

40. The most likely first alcoholic beverage was _____.
    a. Mead
    b. Whiskey
    c. Ale
    d. Wine
    e. Rum

41. If death is caused by inhalants, what is typically the cause?
    a. Brain damage
    b. Aspiration
    c. Cardiac arrest
    d. Pneumonia
    e. Cancer from cell mutations

Use the following for questions 42-46
    I.      Moral Model
    II.     Social Model
    III.    Psychological Model
    IV.     Disease Model
    V.      Temperance Model

42. Focus on drug use being a learned behavior:
    a. I
    b. II
    c. III
    d. IV
    e. V

43. Believes that some people are born with an "addictive personality":
    a. I
    b. II
    c. III
    d. IV
    e. V

44. Believes the idea of moderation is impractical, so abstinence is the best option.
    a. I
    b. II
    c. III
    d. IV
    e. V

45. Believes that drug is a conscious deviance from societal rules and should be punished:
    a. I
    b. II
    c. III
    d. IV
    e. V

46. Believes that drug use is unique, irreversible, and progressive:
    a. I
    b. II
    c. III
    d. IV
    e. V

47. Which of the following is used to treat alcohol abuse?
    a. Methadone
    b. Naloxone
    c. Acetaminophen
    d. Antabuse
    e. Stimulants

48. Which of the following will users sometimes administer to end an amphetamine run?
    a. Aspirin
    b. Barbiturates
    c. Antibiotics
    d. Tobacco
    e. Excessive amounts of caffeine

49. How many warnings are rotated on the packages of cigarettes?
    a. 1
    b. 2
    c. 3
    d. 4
    e. 5

50. Who is typically a user of heroin?
    a. High functioning white-collar men
    b. Children between the ages of 12-17
    c. Homemakers hoping to cure boredom
    d. Terminally ill people for pain
    e. Unemployed people living in unstable conditions

51. The small gap between neurons is the?
    a. Synapse
    b. Synaptic cleft
    c. Dendrites
    d. Glial cells
    e. Axon

52. Which of the following is NOT a risk factor in steroid abuse:
    a. Skin problems
    b. Psychological issues
    c. Increase risk of blood borne pathogens (such as HIV)
    d. Changes in reproductive system
    e. Changes in cardiovascular system

Use the following for questions 53-57
    I.    Sinsemilla
    II.   Ganja
    III.  Hashish
    IV.   Kief
    V.    Ditch weed

53. Produced from the dried tops of female plants:
    a. I
    b. II
    c. III
    d. IV
    e. V

54. High quality marijuana (literally meaning "without seeds"):
    a. I
    b. II
    c. III
    d. IV
    e. V

55. Low quality marijuana:
    a. I
    b. II
    c. III
    d. IV
    e. V

56. Made from resin of the female plant:
    a. I
    b. II
    c. III
    d. IV
    e. V

57. Made in Morocco of only the glandular heads:
    a. I
    b. II
    c. III
    d. IV
    e. V

58. How many steps in the AA program?
    a. 6
    b. 8
    c. 10
    d. 12
    e. 20

59. Which of the following drugs also has a non-drug use (making of clothing) for the plant of which it is derived?
    a. Cannabis sativa
    b. Poppy
    c. Potato
    d. Deadly Night Shade
    e. Coca leaves

60. Alcohol is considered a:
    a. Stimulant
    b. Food
    c. Opioid
    d. Hallucinogenic
    e. Carcinogen

61. Which of the following is a derivative of opium:
    a. Morphine
    b. Mescaline
    c. LSD
    d. Cannabis
    e. Ma huang

Use the following for questions 62-66
    I.    Administration
    II.   Absorption
    III.  Distribution
    IV.   Activation
    V.    Elimination

62. How is the drug metabolized through the system?
    a. I
    b. II
    c. III
    d. IV
    e. V

63. How does the drug move throughout parts of the body?
    a. I
    b. II
    c. III
    d. IV
    e. V

64. How does the drug move from initial intake to the part of the body it is supposed to effect?
    a. I
    b. II
    c. III
    d. IV
    e. V

65. How the drug is used to produce an effect?
    a. I
    b. II
    c. III
    d. IV
    e. V

66. How is the drug introduced to body?
    a. I
    b. II
    c. III
    d. IV
    e. V

67. State-dependent learning is associated with which of the following substances?
    a. Tobacco
    b. Alcohol
    c. Stimulants
    d. Opioids
    e. OTC drugs

68. The metabolism of alcohol takes place mainly in the _____,
    a. Kidneys
    b. Hypothalamus
    c. Pancreas
    d. Bladder
    e. Liver

69. Of the following which is NOT a function of the glial cells?
   a. Surrounding neurons holding them in place
   b. Providing a mechanism of communication between neurons
   c. Insulating neurons from one another
   d. Destroying pathogens
   e. Removing dead neurons

Use the following for questions 70-74
   I.     Natural
   II.    Fully-synthetic
   III.   Semi-synthetic
   IV.    Endogenous
   V.     Not an opiate

70. Cocaine is an example of _____.
   a. I
   b. II
   c. III
   d. IV
   e. V

71. Endorphins are an example of _____ opiates.
   a. I
   b. II
   c. III
   d. IV
   e. V

72. Morphine is what kind of opiate?
   a. I
   b. II
   c. III
   d. IV
   e. V

73. Heroin is what kind of opiate?
   a. I
   b. II
   c. III
   d. IV
   e. V

74. Methadone is what kind of opiate:
    a.  I
    b.  II
    c.  III
    d.  IV
    e.  V

75. Which of the following is an example of drug misuse?
    a.  Sharing a prescription
    b.  Stopping a medicine before it is prescribed
    c.  Unintentionally taking more of an OTC drug than prescribed
    d.  All of the above
    e.  None of the above, there is no such thing as drug misuse. There is only drug abuse and drug addiction.

76. Which drug use explanation subscribes to the belief that genetics are partially responsible for a person's drug use:
    a.  Psychological
    b.  Bejerots Addiction to Pleasure Theory
    c.  Biological
    d.  Social
    e.  There is no reputable theory that believes genetics is partially responsible for drug use.

77. The most commonly abused drug in the United States is:
    a.  Marijuana
    b.  Heroin
    c.  Alcohol
    d.  Cocaine
    e.  Steroids

78. Which of the following is not a sign of acute alcohol poisoning?
    a.  Flushed cheeks
    b.  Weak and rapid pulse
    c.  Clammy skin
    d.  Bluish tint to the skin
    e.  Asphyxiation from choking on vomit

79. If someone says they are able to "taste a song" what are they experiencing?
   a. Hallucination
   b. Delusion
   c. Paranoia
   d. Synesthesia
   e. Schizophrenia

80. Which of the following is TRUE about tobacco use?
   a. Ancestry makes a difference
   b. Women smoke more than men
   c. College graduates are more likely to smoke
   d. Whites are more likely to use smokeless tobacco
   e. Drinkers have the same likeliness to smoke as non-drinkers

81. The drug having the most dangerous immediate threat of death is _____.
   a. Inhalants
   b. Hallucinogens
   c. Stimulants
   d. Alcohol
   e. Sedative hypnotics

82. Buerger's disease is caused by:
   a. Alcohol
   b. Tobacco
   c. Heroin
   d. Stimulants
   e. Hallucinogens

83. The South American Indians living in Andean were known to consume what product:
   a. Coca leaves
   b. Deadly Nightshade
   c. Cannabis Sativa
   d. Mead
   e. Tea leaves

84. Opium is derived from what part of the plant?
    a.  Pollen
    b.  Petals
    c.  Stems
    d.  Dried sap
    e.  Leaves closest to the flower

85. Cocaine use has been shown to increase the risk of:
    a.  Cancer
    b.  Cirrhosis
    c.  HIV
    d.  Gout
    e.  Renal failure

86. The use of several types of steroids in sequence is called?
    a.  Pyramiding
    b.  Cycling
    c.  Stacking
    d.  Plateauing
    e.  Building blocks

87. Fermented alcoholic beverages of a maximum alcoholic content of approximately:
    a.  15%
    b.  20%
    c.  30%
    d.  5%
    e.  18%

88. Which o the following is NOT a reason people use inhalants?
    a.  Easy to hide
    b.  Accessible
    c.  Able to maintain a functional high
    d.  Cheap
    e.  Don't understand the dangers

89. Which of the following is NOT a legal reason to administer opiates?
   a. Anti-diarrheal
   b. Cough suppressants
   c. Pain relief
   d. Combat situations
   e. Depression

90. The active ingredient in peyote is _____.
   a. Pescaline
   b. Cannabis Sativa
   c. Psilocybin
   d. Psilocin
   e. Mescaline

91. Which drug is associated with amotivational syndrome?
   a. Tobacco
   b. Caffeine
   c. Opiods
   d. Cannabis
   e. Hallucinogens

92. Someone who tries cocaine once but doesn't believe identify him or herself as a drug addict is displaying what behavior?
   a. Labeling
   b. Master status
   c. Temperance
   d. Primary deviance
   e. Secondary deviance

93. All of the following are examples of a Master Status except?
   a. Druggie
   b. Mental patient
   c. Alcoholic
   d. Pastor
   e. Brunette

94. Which of the following is an herbal stimulant?
    a.  Echinacea
    b.  Ginkgo biloba
    c.  St. John's wort
    d.  Milk thistle
    e.  Ma huang

95. How do children in the United States get most of their caffeine intake?
    a.  Tea
    b.  Soda
    c.  Chocolate
    d.  Coffee shops
    e.  Red Bull

96. Assuming diet/exercise remains the same what is likely to happen with the introduction of alcohol?
    a.  Weight loss
    b.  Weight gain
    c.  Vitamin deficiency
    d.  Increased appetite
    e.  Diabetes

97. Which of the following is the least likely administration of tobacco products in the United States?
    a.  Cigarettes
    b.  Cigars
    c.  Chew
    d.  Dip
    e.  Snuff

98. Which drug type is known for flashbacks?
    a.  Alcohol
    b.  Tobacco
    c.  Hallucinogens
    d.  Stimulants
    e.  Inhalants

99. The half-life of a dose of cocaine is about:
    a. Fifteen minutes
    b. Thirty minutes
    c. One hour
    d. One day (24 hours)
    e. One week

100. What is the active ingredient in cacti (peyote) that produces hallucinations?
    a. Psilocybin
    b. Psilocin
    c. Mescaline
    d. Phencyclidine
    e. Ketamine

## ANSWER KEY

1. A. When hallucinogens were outlawed the Native American church had an exception.

2. D. Identifying someone as a doctor, lawyer or drug addict is an example of his or her master status.

3. E. Total relaxation is not an effect of a hallucinogen.

4. A. The three distinct stages of stimulant withdrawal are: crash, withdrawal, and extinction.

5. C. Psychological is not one of the ways that users experience the consumption of a substance.

6. A. United States beer has the smallest alcohol content.

7. E. Due to the 1994 federal regulation there is little the government can do to intervene upon the sales of herbal supplements.

8. C. FAS is not exhibited by a flat face and upper slant of the eye (those are signs of down syndrome).

9. B. Naloxone is used to treat a heroin overdose.

10. E. Dilated pupils are not a side effect of anti-psychotics.

11. E. They are all club drugs.

12. A. St. John's Wort is sometimes used to treat depression.

13. A. Prohibition did not have its intended effect. Criminal activity (such as bootlegging) soared through underground channels (such as speakeasies).

14. A. Nausea occurs when someone drinks under the influence of Antabuse.

15. B. The buildup of a drug in the body after multiple doses in short intervals is the cumulative effect.

16. A. Homeostasis is the bodies desire for stability.

17. B. A blunt is marijuana rolled in cigar paper.

18. E. Ma huang is an herbal stimulant.

19. A. Echinacea is used as a general cure-all.

20. D. Milk thistle is used to treat cuts and burns.

21. C. Ginko Biloba is used to improve memory.

22. B. Saint John's Wort is used to treat depression.

23. B. Dendrites are the branchlike structures that pick up communications for neurons.

24. D. Environmental factors do not play a role in BAC.

25. B. Ethanol is grain alcohol.

26. C. Barbiturates are Schedule III drugs.

27. B. Schedule II drugs are monitored by the DEA.

28. A. Schedule I drugs are not medically accepted.

29. D. Schedule IV drugs include the sleeping pill choral hydrate.

30. E. Cough suppressants are considered Schedule V drugs.

31. C. Lack of Thiamine causes the Wernicke-Korsakoff syndrome.

32. C. The most widely used illicit drug is marijuana.

33. E. The high-risk groups for inhalants are: young, socioeconomically disadvantaged, incarcerated, and institutionalized.

34. D. Potentiated effect is when one drug intensifies the effect of another.

35. C. SADD focuses on a contractual agreement between parent and child.

36. E. Benzodiazepines are examples of sedative hypnotics and anti-anxiety drugs.

37. E. The spinal cavity, meninges, cerebral cortex, RAS, and brain can all be found in the CNS.

38. B. Sleeping an additional hour a day is not relevant to quitting smoking.

39. C. Anticholinergic hallucinogens are found in the potato family

40. A. The most likely first alcoholic beverage was mead (fermented honey).

41. B. The most likely cause of death from inhalants is aspiration.

42. B. The social model stresses drug use being a learned behavior.

43. C. The psychological model believes that some people are born with an addictive personality that makes them more susceptible to drug use.

44. E. The temperance model subscribes to the belief that moderation is impractical.

45. A. The moral model believes that drug use is a conscious decision and punishable.

46. D. The disease model believes that drug use is unique, irreversible, and progressive.

47. D. Antabuse is used to treat alcoholics.

48. B. Barbiturates are sometimes used to end an amphetamine run.

49. D. Four warnings are rotated on the cigarette packaging.

50. E. Unemployed people living in unstable conditions would be most likely to use heroin.

51. B. The synaptic cleft is the small gap between neurons.

52. C. Increased risk of HIV is not a side-effect of steroid abuse

53. B. Ganja is made of the dried up heads of female plants.

54. A. Sinsemilla is high quality marijuana that is made without seeds.

55. E. Ditch weed is a low quality marijuana

56. C. Hashish is made of the marijuana resin.

57. D. Keif is Moroccan marijuana made of glandular heads.

58. D. There are 12 steps in the AA program.

59. A. Cannabis sativa is also the source of hemp used for clothing and rope.

60. B. Because alcohol is a source of caloric intake it is also considered a food.

61. A. Morphine is a derivative of opium.

62. E. Elimination is how the drug metabolizes in the body.

63. C. Distribution is how the drug moves through the body.

64. B. Absorption is how the drug moves from administration to activation.

65. D. Activation is how the drug is used to produce an effect.

66. A. Administration is how the drug is introduced into the body.

67. C. State dependent learning is associated with stimulants.

68. E. Liver is largely responsible for metabolizing alcohol.

69. B. Glial cells are not responsible for communication between neurons.

70. E. Cocaine is not an opiate.

71. D. Endorphins are endogenous opiates.

72. A. Morphine is a natural opiate.

73. C. Heroin is a semi-synthetic opiate.

74. B. Methadone is a fully synthetic opiate.

75. D. All of the above. Drug misuse exists when someone shares their prescription, unintentionally takes more OTC drugs than directed, or stops a medication before they are prescribed to do so.

76. C. The Biological perspective on drug use opines that genetics are partially responsible for drug abuse.

77. C. The most commonly abused drug in the United States is alcohol.

78. A. Flushed cheeks are not signs of alcohol poisoning.

79. D. Synesthesia is the mixing of the senses.

80. D. Whites are more likely to use smokeless tobacco.

81. A. Inhalants pose the most immediate death threat to a user.

82. B. Buerger's disease is caused by tobacco products.

83. A. South American Andean Indians consumed Coca leaves (cocaine).

84. D. Opium is derived from the dried sap of the poppy.

85. C. Cocaine has been known to increase the risk of HIV because people are more risky with sexual activity and share needles.

86. B. Cycling is using several types of steroids in sequence.

87. A. Fermented alcoholic beverages of a maximum alcoholic content of approximately 15%.

88. C. People do not use inhalants for a functional high.

89. E. Opiates are not used legitimately to treat depression.

90. E. Mescaline is the active ingredient in peyote.

91. D. Cannabis is associated with amotivational syndrome.

92. D. Primary deviance is when someone is performing a deviant behavior but does not identify him or herself with it.

93. E. A brunette is not an example of a master status that is a characteristic.

94. E. Ma huang is an herbal stimulant.

95. B. Children in the United States consume most of their caffeine through soda.

96. B. Alcohol contains empty calories. Therefore, with the introduction of alcohol weight gain is probable.

97. E. Snuff is the least likely used tobacco product in the United States.

98. C. Hallucinogens are known for flashbacks.

99. C. The half-life of cocaine is about an hour.

100. C. Mescaline is the active ingredient in peyote.

Master status, 140, 150, 169
mature out, 99
MDA. *See* methylenedioxyamphetamine
MDMA, 21, 67, 114, 132, 152
mead, 29, 175
medicines, 10, 140
meninges, 23, 174
methadone maintenance, 90
methamphetamine, 66, 71, 72, 140
methylenedioxyamphetamine, 67
milk thistle, 112, 152, 170, 173
minnesota model, 45, 141
monamine oxidase inhibitors, 118
mood stabilizers. *See* Antidepressants
moon rocks, 89
moral model, 15, 175
Mothers Against Drunk Driving (MADD), 44, 141

**N**

naloxone, 89
narcotics, 11, 15, 19
nerve impulse, 25
neurons, 23, 24, 25, 141, 147, 148, 161, 165, 173, 176, 177
neurotransmitters, 12, 25, 58, 119, 136
nicotine, 58, 64, 67, 110, 122, 142
nitrites, 54
nitrous oxide, 53, 54, 142
norepinephrine, 25, 118

**O**

Ogata, Akira, 66
opioids, 78, 122, 164
opium, 82, 83, 168, 178
over-the-counter drugs, 10

**P**

passive smoking, 64, 142
Percocet, 80, 115
Percodan, 80
peripheral nervous system, 23, 24
pethidine, 81
pituitary gland, 108
potency, 26
primary deviance, 14, 143, 169, 178
problem drinking, 37
prohibition, 29, 152
proof, 29
propoxyphene, 81
psychedelics, 102
psychoactive drugs, 101
psychological explanation, 13
psychological model, 15, 175
pulmonary emphysema, 59, 145

**R**

reactive depression. *See* depression: secondary
reticular activating system, 23
rohypnol, 114, 132, 152

**S**

schizophrenia, 103, 104, 116
secondary deviance, 14, 146, 169
secondhand smoke, 64

Made in the USA
Lexington, KY
12 March 2010